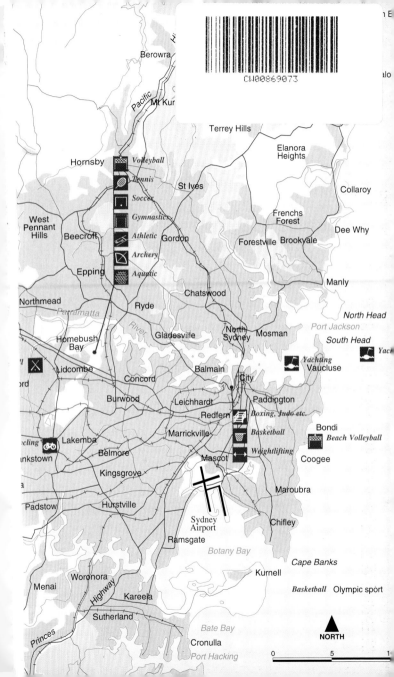

The Pocket Guidebook

SYDNEY

Little Hills Press

DISCLAIMER
Whilst all care has been taken by the publisher and author to ensure that
the information is accurate and up to date, the publisher does not take
responsibility for the information published herein. The
recommendations are those of the author, and as things get better or
worse, places close and others open, some elements in the book may be
inaccurate when you get there. Please write and tell us about it so we can
update in subsequent editions.

Little Hills ^{TM} and ![] are registered trademarks of
Little Hills Press Pty Ltd.

Front Cover: View of the City from the Mosman side of the harbour.
Facing Title Page: Sydney Opera House from Lavendar Bay.
Back Cover: Sydney from Gladesville.

Contents

Introduction

Sydney is the capital city of the State of New South Wales, the birthplace of the Nation of Australia, and the largest city in the country.

It is located on the south-east coast of Australia, latitude 33 53' south, longitude 151 13' east, on the shores of Sydney Harbour, arguably the most beautiful harbour in the world.

Life in this cosmopolitan city is geared to outdoor activities, taking advantage of the long hours of sunshine and the moderate climate.

Climate

Sydney has a temperate climate, and the average temperatures are: January max 26C - min 19C; July max 17C - min 8C.

The Seasons are:

Summer - December through February

Autumn - March through May

Winter - June through August

Spring - September through November.

The average annual rainfall is 1216mm, with the heaviest falls in the period from February to July. Sydney does not experience snow nor sleet, and quite often the temperature on a winter's day is higher than that of London or San Francisco in the middle of their summers.

What to wear

Lightweight clothing is necessary for the summer months, and medium to heavy for the winter months. A raincoat, or at least an umbrella, should be included in your suitcase whatever the season.

People

The population of Sydney is around 3,800,000, more than half that of the entire State of New South Wales, and it would be hard to think of an ethnic group that is not represented in that number.

Australians speak English, and apart from a few differently pronounced words, the accent is the same in Sydney as in any other city in the country.

Fishing off Mrs. Macquarie's Point

History

Although many Europeans visited the vast continent of Australia during the 17th and 18th centuries, the honour of discovery goes to Captain James Cook, who sailed into Botany Bay on April 29, 1770. He landed and raised the Union Jack at a spot now known as Kurnell, taking possession of the whole eastern coast in the name of King George III, and calling it New South Wales.

The powers that be in England ignored their new possession until 1786, when they were trying to decide where to relocate the growing number of convicts they could no longer send to independent America. The botanist from the Cook expedition, Joseph Banks, had been suggesting for years that they be sent to New South Wales, and finally Captain Arthur Phillip, RN, was ordered to establish a penal colony at Botany Bay.

First Fleet

The First Fleet set sail on May 13, 1787, and comprised HMS *Sirius*, the armed tender *Supply*, three storeships and six transports, with food, clothing and other supplies for two years. The ships also carried 1044 people, comprising 568 male and 191 female convicts with 13 children; 206 marines with 27 wives and 19 children; and 20 officials. The fleet anchored in Botany Bay, but could not find a source of fresh water, so they continued their journey north and sailed into Port Jackson (Sydney Harbour) on January 26, 1788. Fresh water was discovered, and work on the new settlement began the next day, when the convicts from the *Scarborough* began clearing trees.

The local Aborigines called the area *Warrane*[1], but this name didn't suit the British, who had thought of calling

[1]   The name also given in the 1960s to perhaps the most prestigious university residential college in the country - Warrane College - at the University of New South Wales.

the new settlement Albion. Phillip, however, had other ideas, and named the inlet in honour of his patron, Baron Sydney of Chiselhurst. The original name was actually Sydney Cove, but general usage tended to drop the word 'Cove' and everyone simply called it 'Sydney'. Sydney Cove still exists as a location on maps and charts, although its outline has changed drastically from the original, and Sydneysiders now refer to it as 'The Quay'.

The freshwater stream, called 'Tank Stream', is still in existence, but it now flows beneath a modern city. Bridge Street, which runs roughly parallel to Alfred Street (Circular Quay), gets its name because it was the track that crossed Tank Stream. Nevertheless the settlement survived and grew. Intrepid explorers discovered vast areas of fertile land and small satellite settlements were formed, the first at Parramatta, 24km west of Sydney.

The infant colony was not without its problems:

* The soil, except for a small area in what is now the Botanical Gardens, was found to be of inferior quality.

* The majority of convicts were city people, with no experience of farming.

* And the government in Britain was very good at giving orders as to what was to be done, but not very good at understanding the colony's problems, or in giving assistance. They simply kept sending more convicts, thereby putting more strain on supplies.

1800s
The hardships of the early years of the colony gave way to the prosperity of the mid1800s with the discovery of rich lands to the west of the Great Dividing Range which could support masss farming to provide the colony with its food need. By 1842, with the constant arrivals of more convicts and free-settlers, the colony had grown to more that 30,000 people and it was in this same year that Sydney was declared a city. By 1848, the British ceased sending convicts to Sydney, but the colony continued attracting free-settlers, desperate to escape the poverty and hardship of the British Isles. With the discovery of gold in the 1850s on the other side of the Blue Mountains,

Sydney developed into a prosperous town.

Building Sydney - late 1800s
In the latter half of the 1800s, grand developments began in some way to make Sydney almost an elegant showplace of Victorian architecture with a number of impressive buildings being constructed. St Mary's Cathedral and St Andrew's, the Great Synagogue, Town Hall, Victoria Barracks, the Great Post Office and Sydney University - all of which still survive today - were some of the projects.

Economic depression hit the city in the 1890s when it boasted of a population of 383,000 and then again in 1929 when it had grown to over a million inhabitants.

The Harbour Bridge
Scenes of hardship were worse than every imagined with as the economy crumbled in the early 1930s. Shanty towns sprang up on the edge of the city and dole queues became a regular sight. It was during this period that the harbour bridge was built - beginning in 1922 and opening in March 1932. The bridge became the city's proudest land mark. The bridge was known during the Depression as the 'Iron Lung' since it literally saved many families from starving because of the number of people involved in its construction. It is therefore no wonder that in the gloomy days of the depression when Sydney did not have a lot of bright things happening to it, the bridge was dubbed 'the bridge of our Dreams'.

Second World War
With the outbreak of hostilities in 1939 and with Japanese forces so close to Australia, Sydney was thought to be a major target. The city soon found itself overrun with US Service personnel, either stationed here or on leave. They brought new styles and ways of life to the, until then, provincial city. The war became a reality to Sydney when in May 1942 three Japanese midget submarines entered Sydney Harbour and caused havoc. Though in the end, the toll was relatively light, with an old ferry used as a

barrack ship being sunk killing nineteen sailors. Two submarines were destroyed but the third was never recovered. A week later, Sydney was again under attack when coastal suburbs were shelled by a Japanese warship.

Migration

Following the war, in the late 1940s and '50s Sydney received an influx of people from all over the world migrating to Australia to start a new life after war had ravaged their home countries. Sydney grew once more and suburbs began developing to accommodate the influx of new people. The city began to sprawl along the main transport corridors-the train lines and major highways-and new communities developed.

1960s

With the change in attitude to social and moral standards, the 1960s was a great period of change for Sydney. Certain areas of the city began attracting particular minority groups and places like Kings Cross, once the bohemian and cosmopolitan side of Sydney became its sleaze face, littered with sex shops, massage parlours, seedy nightclubs and open prostitution. This rapid change was brought on with the presence of American and allied soldiers on leave from fighting in the Vietnam conflict. The area is seedier than ever and is not safe at night - something unheard of years ago.

1970s to the present

New changes took place in Sydney in the late 1960s and '70s with the redevelopment of large parts of the city. New buildings were planned, more trees planted and more restaurants and tourist sites opened to make the most of the outstanding location of the city as it surrounds a magnificent harbour. Australians like their own home with its garden, and the urban sprawl started north, south and west towards the Blue Mountains. It has yet to abate.

The Opera House

The grandest change to the face of Sydney was the opening of the Opera House on Sydney Harbour in 1973 -

sixteen years and $102 million in the making. Sydney now had a a performing arts centre which has contributed greatly to making the city one of the world's premier cities. Plans for redevelopment of the city abounded in the 70s which involved the demolition of historically important areas. Green bans imposed by the Builders' Labourers federation (now defunct) under the leadership of Jack Mundy prevented such a process.

Eventually common sense prevailed and over time places like The Rocks, Queen Victoria Building and the Capitol Theatre have been either enhanced or restored to their former glory.

Olympic Games and the year 2000

Building continues a pace in the Olympic City, which now boasts a population of almost 4 million people. However successive governments of both persuasion have shown remarkably little vision in coping with Sydney's ever increasing traffic problem. However, the container terminals have gone from Sydney Harbour and now the city has a pollution free harbour. Air pollution and aircraft noice are two challenges that are starting to be solved after much public agitation.

Sydney is the epitome of the new world and all the good that comes with it. It is possible to have an english-style breakfast at a French café, go grocery shopping at the corner Greek store, have lunch at a Chinese restaurant, a snack at a Lebanese fast food place, and after seeing an Italian movie go to dinner at a Sushi House.
That's Sydney!

Festivals

The Festival of Sydney is held during the entire month of January each year, and features include twilight and open-air concerts in the Domain, contemporary music at Hyde Park and Darling Harbour, outdoor movies at the Opera House, bike rallies, street theatre, and classical theatre performances at the Opera House, the Belvoir Theatre and the Seymour Centre.

Australia Day, January 26, sees the city come alive, especially around the harbour, with all kinds of displays, and a Ferrython in which all the Sydney ferries compete.

The Royal Easter Show has been held at the Showground in Moore Park for decades, but 1997 will mark its last appearance at that site. The 1998 Show will be held at Homebush Bay, the venue for the 2000 Olympics.

The Show normally begins on the Friday before Good Friday and finishes on Easter Tuesday.

Advertised as "when the country comes to town", there's something for everyone, with displays of horticulture, livestock, crafts and hi-tech machinery. For kids, there are rides and sample bags, and for all ages there is non-stop entertainment in the show ring with livestock judging, trotting races, equestrian events, the Grand Parade, bands, sky divers, clowns, rodeos, and fireworks displays.

The Show is well patronised by Sydneysiders with attendances on the public holidays reaching 100,000.

The **National Folkloric Festival** is an annual multicultural event featuring dancers and musicians from many ethnic backgrounds. It is held in June, and begins with a Sunday parade that terminates at the Opera House, the scene for the many events of the following weekend.

The Biennale of Sydney is an international exhibition of contemporary art held every two years. Since its inception in 1973, the Biennale has brought the world's leading artists to Sydney, and more than 800 of them from over 45 countries have been exhibited.

The Biennale is not only confined to Sydney as visiting artists travel giving lectures, workshops and artist -in-residence programs, and special lectures and displays are organised.

The Sydney to Hobart Yacht Race can hardly be classed as a festival, but it does generate a lot of excitement. Every Boxing Day thousands of people line the vantage spots around the harbour to watch the mini and maxi yachts set off on their adventure, and there are so many boats of all sorts on the harbour, farewelling the entrants, that it is a wonder they ever get through the Heads. The race is closely monitored by news crews in light aircraft, and hourly reports are given on TV and radio as to who is in the lead, and by how much. Meanwhile, the people in Hobart get ready for the big welcoming party.

The City to Surf Fun Run is another annual event. Held every year in August, thousands of people of all ages assemble for the start of the run to Bondi Beach, and as the starting gun goes off, Park Street becomes a sea of people. Of course, the race is always won by a professional marathon runner, but winning is not really what the spectacle is all about. Everyone who finishes receives a certificate, and their names are listed in the newspapers. Even those who don't finish are congratulated for entering, and there is a real spirit of comradeship as you watch people helping each other along the way.

The Gay Mardi Gras is organised by a combination of gay and lesbian groups and is now held on the first Friday in February each year. It is actually part of a month long festival that centres around the Oxford Street section of the city. It is not without its critics with the focus of the activities being the gay Mardi Gras parade full of much noise, colour and sights. If you are into watching cavorting tits and bums then this is the place to be. Gays from interstate and overseas decend on Sydney, and the organisers seem to feel the need to overestimate the crowd that watches this spectacle. It usually attracts about 30,000. Oxford Street is best avoided if you have your own car, especially the next day.

In addition to the above, each municipal area of Sydney has its own festival, and there are other special annual events, such as the blessing of the fishing fleet.

Public Holidays

Christmas, Boxing Day, New Year and Easter are obviously celebrated at the same time as everywhere else in the world.

Other holidays that are enjoyed in Australia are:

Australia Day - January 26.

Anzac Day - April 25.

Queen's Birthday - the second Monday in June.

Labour Day - the first Monday in October.

Another day is *Bank Holiday*, which is held on the first Monday in August, but only banks, government offices, insurance companies and the like are closed.

Travel Tips

Airport Facilities

Kingsford-Smith International Airport is situated in the suburb of Mascot, 10km from the city centre. The Domestic Terminals are 3km to the east of the Overseas, and are connected by taxis and express buses. The buses run every 20 minutes, 7 days a week, and the one-way fares are $5 adults, $3 children. The Route 400 Bus (see below) also includes travel between the terminals in its normal trip, and the fares are $2.50 adults, $1.25 children.

The airport has all the facilities expected of a modern international airport - money changing, information, hotel bookings, shops, cafes, bars, restrooms, showers, etc.

Transport from the Airport

The State Transit Airport Express has a service every 10 minutes from the Airport to Central Railway Station.
Bus Route 300 travels between the Airport and Circular Quay, stopping at specially-identified places along George Street and in Eddy Avenue near Central Station.

Route 350 travels between the Airport and Elizabeth Bay, passing through Kings Cross.

The services run 7 days a week, and the fares are one-way adults $5, children $3, return ticket is $8 and the return journey can be taken up to 60 days after the initial trip.

Other Sydney Buses routes that travel via the airport are *Route 100* (Dee Why-Airport, every 30 minutes Mon-Fri), *Route 305* (Railway Square-Airport, every 30 minutes Mon-Fri) and *Route 400* (Bondi Junction-Airport-Burwood, every 20 minutes Mon-Fri, every 30 minutes Sat-Sun).

Kingsford-Smith Airport Services (KSA) operate a bus service between the Airport, City, Kings Cross and Glebe.

Buses meet all incoming international and major domestic flights. Passengers may alight en route at hotels on request, and transfer time is around 40 minutes.

To arrange a KSA transfer to the Airport, phone one hour in advance. Services run daily every half-hour, 6am-8pm, ph 9667 3221, 9667 0663 or 9667 3800, and the fares are $6 adults, $4 children under 12 years old.

Airline Offices

Following is a selection of airline reservation and flight confirmation telephone numbers.

Qantas - ph 9957 0111.
Air New Zealand - ph 13 24 76.
Canadian Airlines - ph 9299 7843.
British Airways - ph 9258 3300.
Cathay Pacific - ph 13 1747.
Singapore Airlines - ph 13 1011.
United Airlines - ph 13 1777.

Churches and Temples

Because of the multinational population, all religions and sects are present in Sydney. There are parish churches in all the suburbs, but following is a list of churches in the inner city area.

Anglican
St Andrew's Cathedral, George Street (next to the Town Hall), ph 9265 1661.
St James' Church, 173 King Street, ph 9232 3022.
St Philip's Church Hill, 3 York Street, ph 9247 1071.
Christ Church St Laurence, 507 Pitt Street, ph 9211 0560.
Church of The Holy Trinity (The Garrison Church), Argyle & Lower Fort Streets, The Rocks, ph 9247 2664.

Baptist
Central Baptist Church, 619 George Street, ph 9211 1833.

Catholic
St Mary's Cathedral, College & Cathedral Streets, ph 9220 0400.

St Peter Julian's Church, 641 George Street, Haymarket, ph 9211 4100.

St Patrick's Church, Grosvenor Street, ph 9247 3525, 9247 3516 (recorded Mass times).

The Marist Chapel, 5 Young Street, ph 9247 9292.

Sacred Heart Church, Darlinghurst Road, Darlinghurst, ph 9331 2147.

St Francis, 10 Albion Street, Surry Hills, ph 9212 2145.

Jewish

The Great Synagogue, Elizabeth Street, ph 9267 2477.

Lutheran

German Lutheran Church, 96 Goulburn Street, ph 9267 8683.

Central Trinity Lutheran Church, 17 Valentine Street, ph 9211 5983.

St Paul's Lutheran Church, 3 Stanley Street, ph 9331 1822.

Presbyterian

Scots Church, Margaret, York & Jamison Streets, ph 9299 1804.

The Welsh Church, Chalmers Street, Surry Hills, ph 9810 7869.

Salvation Army

Congress Hall Corps, 140 Elizabeth Street, ph 9266 9801.

Communications

Mail

The General Post Office, 159-171 Pitt Street, ph 13 1317, is open Mon-Fri 8.15am-5.30pm, Sat 8.15am-noon.

Suburban post offices are open Mon-Fri 9am-5.30pm.

The postage for mailing a postcard by Air Mail is:

To New Zealand - 70c
    Singapore - 80c
    Hong Kong and Japan - 90c
    United States and Canada - 95c
    United Kingdom - ....$1.00.

(Facing) Part of the National Maritime Museum
(Overleaf) Sydney Harbour at sunrise [top]; Manly Ferry with Bradleys Head lighthouse in foreground.

Telephone

Public telephones are found in hotels, shops and cafes, and on street corners, and a local call costs 40c, irrespective of the length of the call.

Calls to places out of the Sydney 02 Area Code are time-charged, and the fee varies with the distance involved, and the time of day the call is placed. The cheapest time to ring is from 6pm Sat to 8am Mon, or every day from 10pm to 8am, when savings are up to 60% off the daytime rate. Also, within the metropolitan area if you phone from one zone to another it will be time charged, so check the Telstra White Pages before you starting chatting for hours.

The area codes for places outside the Sydney area are found in the back of the A-K White Pages of the Sydney Telephone Book.
Overseas calls can be dialled direct, and the International Access Code is 0011.

The International Direct Dial country and area codes are also found in the back of the A-K White Pages of the Sydney Telephone Book. *The Country Code for Australia is 61.*

Country Direct is a service which enables travellers in Australia to gain direct access to telephone operators in their home country so as to make telephone credit card or reverse charge (collect) calls. *It may be necessary to insert the local call fee to make a Country Direct call.* To find out the number for your country phone Freecall 1800 801 800.

Time Zones

Australian Eastern Standard Time is Greenwich Mean Time + 10 hours. If Daylight Saving is not involved, when it is Noon in Sydney, the following times are applicable:

> Auckland - 2.00pm
> London - 2.00am
> Los Angeles - 6.00pm (previous day)
> New York - 9.00pm (previous day)
> Ottawa - 9.00pm (previous day)

Singapore - 10.00am
Hong Kong - 10.00am
Tokyo - 11.00am
Vancouver - 6.00pm (previous day)

Sydney, and indeed all of New South Wales, has Daylight Saving, and clocks are put forward one hour at 2.00am on the last Sunday in October every year. Australian Eastern Summer Time continues until 2.00am on the last Sunday in March, when clocks are put back one hour.

If you decide to ring home to the Northern Hemisphere when Sydney is not in Daylight Saving, chances are that your country is on Summer Time, so appropriate adjustment must be made to the times mentioned above. It does not make people conducive to accepting the charges for an overseas call if you wake them up at some ungodly hour.

Useful Telephone Numbers
Emergencies - ....Fire, Police, Ambulance - 000
Directory Assistance - ....Local - 013
....Country & Interstate - 0175
....Overseas - 0103
Call enquiries and costs - ....calls within Australia - 012
....Overseas calls - 0102.

Consulates
Over seventy countries have diplomatic representation in Canberra, the Capital City of Australia, but Consuls can be found in the State capitals.

The addresses for those in Sydney are:
Canada: Level 5, 111 Harrington Street, ph 9364 3000.
Great Britain: Level 16, 1 Macquarie Place, ph 9247 7521.
Japan: 52 Martin Place, ph 9231 3455.
New Zealand: 1 Alfred Street, Circular Quay,
ph 9247 1999.
United States: 39 Castlereagh Street (cnr Martin Place),
ph 9234 9200.

Credit Cards

American Express, Diners, Visa and MasterCard are widely accepted.

Shops and restaurants have the logos of the cards they accept near the front door, or at the check out.

Phone numbers to ring in the event of loss or theft of cards are:

American Express - Cards, 9886 0666
Travellers Cheques, 9886 0689
(after business hours, 9886 0688

Diners Club - 1800 331 199

Mastercard - ANZ Bank - 1800 033 84
Citibank - 13 2484
Commonwealth Bank - 13 2221
(after hours 1800 011 217)
National Bank - 1800 033 103
State Bank (National) - 13 1818
Westpac Bank - 1800 230 144
Bank of Qld - 1800 077 024
R & I Bank of WA - 1800 999 273
International cards - 9248 6100

Visa - Australian cards - 1800 033 844
International cards - 1800 805 341

Dress

The dress code is mostly smart casual. Although the 'typical' Aussie man is thought to spend his life attired in shorts, singlet top and thongs, he would not be allowed in any of the licensed clubs unless he changed to a shirt with a collar, and long pants, or at least dress shorts and long socks. Restaurants consider long pants a necessity, and a few demand the addition of a tie. For women, it is the same as the rest of the world - the more upmarket the venue, the more upmarket the gear you wear.

Electricity

Domestic supply throughout Australia is 230-251 volts, AC50 cycles. Three-pin plugs are fitted to domestic appliances, so 110 appliances, such as hairdryers and contact lens sterilisers, cannot be used without a transformer.

Many of the hotels and motels have adaptor plugs.

Entry Formalities

All travellers to Australia need a valid passport, and visitors of all nationalities except New Zealand, must obtain a visa before arrival. These are available at Australian Embassies, High Commissions and Consular offices listed in local telephone directories. No vaccinations are required.

Each incoming traveller over the age of 18 is allowed duty free goods to the value of $400 plus one litre of liquor and 200 cigarettes.

Exit Formalities

There is a departure tax of $27 for everyone over the age of 12 years who is leaving the country by air. This amount is added to the price of the ticket, so there is no necessity to buy stamps as was once the case.

Health

Sydney has excellent health services, but they are not free. It is essential for visitors to take out insurance before they leave home.

The water is safe to drink, and all foods and fruit can be safely eaten by all.

Information

The *Travellers Information Service* at the Airport can make accommodation bookings, and also has a telephone information service that operates 7 days a week between 8am and 6pm, ph 9669 5111.

First stop in Sydney for all visitors should be the *Travel Centre of New South Wales*, 11-31 York Street, ph 13 2077.

The office is open Mon-Fri 9am-5pm, and has numerous brochures, maps, etc. and a large and very helpful staff. Pick up copies of all the current city information guides and you will have plenty of reading material, and good tips on what to see and where to go.

The *Sydney Tower Visitors Information and Booking Service* is located at the top of the tower, ph 9229 7430. It is open 7 days, 9.30am-9.30pm (Sat till 11.30pm), and is a minefield of information for those people brave enough to take the lift to the top of the tower.

The *Sydney Convention and Visitors Bureau* has an information kiosk in Martin Place which is open Mon-Fri 9am-5pm, ph 9235 2424.

The Rocks Visitor Information Centre, 106 George Street, The Rocks, is open 7 days, 9am-5pm, ph 9255 1788.

Licensing Laws
The legal age for purchasing alcohol is 18 years. Children are permitted into lounge bars where food is served as long as they are accompanied by an adult. Many hotels have outside 'beer gardens' and children are allowed entry to these.

The licensed clubs have their restaurants situated in such a way that children can enter them without passing through any of the bars or gambling areas.

The legal limit of blood alcohol while driving is 0.05 mg/litre.

Media
Newspapers
Sydney has three daily newspapers **Mon-Sat:** the national paper, *The Australian* - $1.00 (the Saturday edition is called *The Weekend Australian* - $1.30); *The Sydney Morning Herald* - 90c (the Saturday edition is $1.50); *The Telegraph* - 80c (the Saturday edition is $1.00).

On Sunday, the choice is between *The Sun-Herald* -$1 and *The Sunday Telegraph* - $1.

For information on entertainment venues, including cinema, theatre and TV programs, and what is happening on the music scene, both modern and classical, there are weekly liftouts in the daily newspapers. The Thursday edition of the *The Telegraph* has "7 Days" and the Friday edition of *The Sydney Morning Herald* has "Metro".

There are also a few free magazines that advertise what is happening around town music-wise - *On the Street (OTS)*, *The Drum Media* and *Beat*. These are available from music and record shops.

Every suburb has at least one local paper that is delivered free to every household, and has news of local interest and happenings.

Radio
Probably the most popular rock music stations are 2MMM (104.9) and 2 Day FM (104.1), and for classical music ABC FM (92.9) and 2MBS FM (102.5). Another FM station with a strong following is Triple J (105.7), which is run by the ABC and broadcast Australia-wide, but sometimes the humour is a trifle black and over the top.

There are also many AM stations that specialise in talk-back or middle of the road music, but these tend to appeal to the older age groups.

Tourist Radio
SYI-FM 87.8 Sydney Inforadio broadcasts in and around central Sydney and gives the latest information on what to see and what to do. Covers visitor services, attractions, accommodation and entertainment.

Television
Sydney has four commercial channels - ATN7, TCN9, TEN10 and SBS (the multicultural network) - and the government owned ABC2. Recently cable television has come to some suburbs, but it is still in its infancy and the programs are mostly re-runs of old series, though Foxtel (Murdoch owned) is starting to corner the Sports market and so is causing some adverse comment among those interested in their rugby and cricket.

Money

Australia uses a decimal currency system with 100 cents equalling one dollar. The notes are in denominations of $100, $50, $20, $10, $5, and coins are $2, $1, 50 cents, 20 cents, 10 cents and 5 cents. The notes come in different sizes and colours, according to denomination, and are made of plastic instead of the usual paper.

Opening Times

Most banks change travellers cheques and foreign currencies, and bank trading hours are Mon-Thurs 9.30am-4pm, Fri 9.30am-5pm, but the major banks in the city area are open Mon-Fri 8.15am-6pm. Also, in the large suburban shopping centres some banks are open until 8pm on Thursdays, and 9.30am-noon on Saturdays.

Outside Banking Hours

Outside banking hours, travellers cheques and foreign currencies can be exchanged at the following Bureaux de Change:

Circular Quay, Jetty Six, ph 9247 2082 - open daily 8am-9.30pm

Infostar, near MCA, Circular Quay, ph 9241 2903 - open daily 8am-9.30pm.

Pitt Street Mall, ph 9233 7159 - open Mon-Fri 9am-6pm (Thurs until 8.30pm), Sat-Sun 9am-5.30pm.

Darling Harbour, ph 9281 3234 - open daily 9am-8.30pm.

Thomas Cook's Currency Exchange Centres are located at: *175 Pitt Street*, ph 9231 2523 - open Mon-Fri 8.45am-5.15pm, Sat 10am-2pm.

The Queen Victoria Building, Shop 22, ph 9264 1133 - open Mon-Fri 8.30am-6pm (Thurs till 9pm), Sat 9am-6pm, Sun & public holidays (except Christmas and Easter) 11am-5pm.

Kings Cross, Hyatt Kingsgate Hotel (top of William Street), ph 9356 2211 - open Mon-Fri 8.45am-5.15pm, Sat 9am-1pm.

Department stores will only accept travellers cheques

that are in Australian currency, as will some small stores in the tourist areas.

Smoking

Sydney is fast becoming a 'Smoke Free Zone' and it will soon be possible to smoke only in the confines of one's own home.

Theatres and cinema complexes do not allow smoking on their premises; the great majority of restaurants have a 'no smoking' section, and some have banned smoking completely; all government buildings and banks are smoke free; the larger hotels have 'no smoking' floors, the smaller have smoke free rooms; the Domestic and the International Airports are cluttered with 'No Smoking' signs; and smoking is forbidden on all flights. The list goes on. The government is doing its bit to help by regularly increasing the tax on tobacco to the point where the price of cigarettes is becoming prohibitive in itself.

If you are one of the dwindling band of nicotine addicts, grab a carton in the duty free shop on arrival, and see if you can make it last for the length of your stay.

Tipping

Tipping is not a way of life 'Down Under'. Of course, if you are particularly impressed by the service you have been given, it is OK to tip. If you decide not to, however, you will not be harassed as you would be in some other countries. It is entirely up to you.

Some restaurants add a small percentage to their bills for weekend trading, and some set a minimum account level. The latter is usually to make sure that customers purchase food as well as beverages, and the limit is usually set at the price of the lowest priced meal.

Accommodation

Sydney has a wide range of accommodation, from luxurious 5-star hotels such as The Intercontinental and The Regent, to small budget-priced establishments offering the basics.

There is now a 7% bed tax imposed on all major city hotels by the State Government whom these days seems to have great difficulty working their finances effectively.

As with most large cities, accommodation is usually cheaper in the suburbs. Following is a selection with prices in Australian dollars for a double room per night, which should be used as a guide only.

The Telephone Area Code is 02.

City Accommodation

Hotels

5-Star

Park Hyatt Sydney, 7 Hickson Road, The Rocks, ph 9241 1234 - 5 suites, 158 rooms, licensed restaurants, cocktail lounge, heated swimming pool, spa, sauna, gym - $490-3000.

Sheraton on the Park, 161 Elizabeth Street, ph 9286 6000 - 50 suites, 561 rooms, licensed restaurants, cocktail lounges, heated swimming pool, sauna, gym - $325-395.

The Ritz-Carlton Sydney, 93 Macquarie Street, ph 9252 4600 - 13 suites, 106 rooms, licensed restaurants, cocktail lounge, heated swimming pool, sauna, gym - $229-309.

The Observatory, 89 Kent Street, ph 9256 2222 - 22 suites, 56 rooms, licensed restaurants, cocktail lounges, heated swimming pool, spa, sauna, gym - $220-246.

ANA Hotel Sydney, 176 Cumberland Street, The Rocks, ph 9250 6000 - 40 suites, 573 rooms, licensed restaurants, cocktail lounges, heated swimming pool, spa, sauna, gym - $200-295.

Hotel Inter-Continental Sydney, 117 Macquarie Street, ph 9230 0200 - 42 suites, 498 rooms, licensed restaurants, cocktail lounges, heated swimming pool, sauna, gym - $205-245.

Hotel Nikko Darling Harbour, 161 Sussex (cnr Sussex St), ph 9299 1231, 645 rooms, licensed restaurants, cocktail bars, pub- Dundee Arms, , gym - $290.

Renaissance Sydney Hotel, 30 Pitt Street, ph 9372 2233 - 579 rooms, 2 licensed restaurants, 2 cocktail bars including the Customs House Bar (Here is where all the 'yuppies' gather from the finance and law industries to drink on a Friday afternoon after work as this bar fronts a rather pleasant park.), fitness centre with heated pool, sauna - $325-$450 (suite).

Regent Hotel, 199 George Street, ph 9238 0000 - 10 suites, 584 rooms, licensed restaurants, cocktail bar, pub bar, heated outdoor swimming pool - a nice big one, sauna - $290-$550.

4-Star

Sheraton Wentworth Sydney, 61 Phillip Street, ph 9230 0700 - 46 suites, 377 rooms, licensed restaurants, cocktail lounges, sauna gym - $220-450.

Sydney Hilton, 259 Pitt Street, ph 9266 0610 - 28 suites, 585 rooms, licensed restaurants, cocktail bars, heated swimming pool, spa, sauna, gym - $260-350.

Old Sydney Parkroyal, 55 George Street, The Rocks, ph 9252 0524 - 174 rooms, licensed restaurant, cocktail lounge, swimming pool, spa, sauna - $290.

Parkroyal at Darling Harbour, 150 Day Street, ph 9261 1188 - 22 suites, 295 units, licensed restaurant, cocktail lounge - $175-255.

Novotel Sydney on Darling Harbour, 100 Murray Street, Pyrmont, ph 9934 0000 - 24 suites, 530 units, licensed restaurant, cocktail lounge, swimming pool, sauna, gym, tennis - $180-210.

All Seasons Premier Menzies, 14 Carrington Street, ph 9299 1000 - 15 suites, 440 rooms, licensed restaurants, cocktail bars, heated indoor pool, spa, sauna, gym - $165.

Hyde Park Plaza Hotel, 38 College Street, ph 9331 6933 - 47 suites, 135 units, licensed restaurant, cocktail lounge, heated swimming pool, spa, sauna - $155-185 (includes continental breakfast).

Forum the grace hotel, 77 York Street, ph 9272 6888, fax 9299 8189, 382 rooms, 2 licenced restaurants, wine bar, heated swimming pool, 2 spa, sauna, steam room - $175.

3-Star

Harbour Rocks, 34 Harrington Street, The Rocks, ph 9251 8944 - 54 rooms, licensed restaurant, cocktail bar - $116-182.

Park Regis, cnr Castlereagh & Park Streets, ph 9267 6511 - 120 units, swimming pool - $118.

The Cambridge, 212 Riley Street, ph 9212 1111 - 25 suites, 170 units, licensed restaurant, heated indoor pool, sauna - $115-$125.

Castlereagh Inn, 169 Castlereagh Street, ph 9264 2281 - 2 suites, 78 rooms - licensed restaurants - $115.

Oxford Koala Hotel, cnr Oxford & Pelican Streets, ph 9269 0645 - 12 suites, 343 units, licensed restaurant, swimming pool - $90-109.

Hotel Ibis, 70 Murray Street, Pyrmont, ph 9563 0888 - 256 rooms, licensed restaurant, cocktail bar - $165-$185.

2-Star

Mercantile Hotel, 25 George Street, ph 9247 3570 - 24 rooms (15 with private facilities nearby), licensed restaurant - B&B $85-120.

Grand Hotel, 30 Hunter Street, ph 9232 3755 - 18 rooms (no private facilities) - $80.

1-Star

The Lord Nelson Brewery Hotel, cnr Kent & Argyle Streets, The Rocks, ph 9251 4044 - 6 rooms (no private facilities), licensed restaurant - B&LtB $60-100.

Westend, 412 Pitt Street, ph 9211 4822 - 91 rooms, licensed restaurant - $65.

Motels

Hyde Park Inn, 271 Elizabeth Street, ph 9264 6001 - 6 suites, 86 units, licensed restaurant (closed Sun), cocktail lounge - $145-$160.

Wynyard Vista, 7 York Street, ph 9299 3000 - 211 units, unlicensed restaurant - $125-200.

Serviced Apartments

5-Star

Quay West Apartments, 98 Gloucester Street, ph 9240 6000 - 144 suites, licensed restaurant, heated indoor pool, spa, sauna, gym - $270-1300.

The York, 5 York Street, ph 9210 5000 - 99 suites, 34 units - licensed restaurant, heated swimming pool, spa, sauna - $200-300 (suites $200-420).

4-Star

Holiday Inn Park Suites, 16 Oxford Street, ph 9331 7728 - 135 units, licensed restaurant, heated swimming pool, spa, sauna - $195-215.

The Waldorf Apartment Hotel, 57 Liverpool Street, ph 9261 5355 - 65 suites, swimming pool, spa, sauna - $160-280.

Carrington Best Western City Centre Apartments, 57 York Street, ph 9299 6556 - 20 units - $180.

3-Star

Stafford Apartments-Quest Sydney, 75 Harrington Street, The Rocks, ph 9251 6711 - 40 units, swimming pool, spa, sauna, gym - $175.

Savoy Serviced Apartments, cnr King & Kent Streets, ph 9267 9211 - 63 units - $148.

Metro Serviced Apartments, 132 Sussex Street, ph 9290 9200 - 33 units - $125-140.

Suburban Accommodation

The suburbs listed here are within a 10km radius of the city centre.

Hotels/Motels/Serviced Apartments

Artarmon (10km north of the city)

4-Star

Twin Towers Motor Inn, 260 Pacific Highway, ph 9439 1388 - 3 suites, 41 units, licensed restaurant, swimming pool,

- 3 suites, 41 units, licensed restaurant, swimming pool, spa - $105-135.

3-Star
Artarmon Motor Inn, 472 Pacific Highway, ph 9412 1644 - 64 units, licensed restaurant, swimming pool, sauna - $90-125.
Linwood Lodge Motel, 312 Pacific Highway, ph 9439 6333 - 16 units - $55-80.

Ashfield (10km west of the city)
4-Star
Palm Court Motor Inn, 17 Parramatta Road, ph 9797 6111 - 32 units, licensed restaurant - $95-105.
Ashfield's Philip Lodge, 156 Parramatta Road, ph 9797 9411 - 2 suites, 48 units, licensed restaurant, pool - $88-98.
3-Star
Metro Motor Inn, 63 Liverpool Road, ph 9798 0333 - 38 units - $75.

Bondi Beach (8km east of the city)
4-Star
Swiss-Grand All Suite Hotel Bondi Beach, cnr Campbell Parade & Beach Road, ph 9365 5666 - 203 suites, licensed restaurant, heated swimming pool, spa, sauna, gym - $180-470.
City Beach Motor Inn, 99 Curlewis Street, ph 9365 3100 - 25 units, swimming pool - $98-145.

3-Star
Bondi Beachside Inn, 152 Campbell Parade, ph 9130 5311 - 70 units, licensed restaurant - $69-88.
The Alice Motel, 30 Fletcher Street, ph 9130 5231 - 31 units, licensed restaurant, swimming pool - $59-89.

2-Star
Bondi Hotel, 178 Campbell Parade, ph 9130 3271 - 18 suites, 47 rooms, licensed restaurants - $30-95.

Camperdown (5km south of the city)
3-Star
Camperdown Travelodge, 9 Missenden Road, ph 9516 1522 - 136 units, licensed restaurant, swimming pool, sauna, gym - $110.
Camperdown Towers Motel, 144 Mallett Street, ph 9519 5211 - swimming pool - $75-80.

Coogee (8km east of the city)
4-Star
Holiday Inn Coogee Beach, 242 Arden Street, ph 9315 7600 - 207 rooms, licensed restaurant, heated swimming pool, gym, tennis - $185-210.
Coogee Sands Motor Inn, 161 Dolphin Street, ph 9665 8588 - 50 units, licensed restaurant, swimming pool - $75-120.

3-Star
Corban International Motel, 183 Coogee Bay Road, ph 9665 2244 - 38 units, licensed restaurant, swimming pool - $89.
Coogee Bay Hotel, 253 Coogee Bay Road, ph 9665 0000 - 5 suites, 42 rooms, licensed restaurant, **Selinas Night Club** (could be noisy Thurs-Sun) - $74-95.

Budget
Surfside Backpackers Pty Ltd, 186 Arden Street, Coogee, Ph 9315 7888, above McDonald's opposite the Coogee Park. Seems popular, rough and ready. You have to share - 4, 6, 10, 18 bed dormitories - $18.00. Great location

Cremorne (6km north of city)
4-Star
Metropole Hotel, 287 Military Road, ph 9909 8888 - 4 suites, 84 rooms, lounge - $60-120.

Darlinghurst (2km east of the city)
4-Star
Morgans of Sydney Serviced Apartments, 304 Victoria Street, ph 9360 7955 - 26 units, licensed restaurant - B&LtB $104-119.

Camelot Inn, 358A Victoria Street, ph 9331 7555 - 37 units - $88.

Double Bay (4km east of the city)
5-Star
The Ritz-Carlton, 33 Cross Street, ph 9362 4455 - 15 suites, 140 rooms, licensed restaurant, swimming pool, gym - $189-239.

4-Star
Savoy Double Bay Hotel, 41 Knox Street, ph 9326 1411 - 2 suites, 34 units - B&LtB $89-99.

Elizabeth Bay (3km east of the city)
5-Star
Sebel Town House Hotel, 23 Elizabeth Bay Road, ph 9358 3244 - 25 suites, 141 rooms, licensed restaurant, cocktail lounge, heated swimming pool, sauna, gym - $145-165.

4-Star
Gazebo Hotel, 2 Elizabeth Bay Road, ph 9358 1999 - 8 suites, 391 units, licensed restaurant, cocktail lounge, heated swimming pool, sauna - $145-180.
Seventeen Elizabeth Bay Road Serviced Apartments, 17 Elizabeth Bay Road, ph 9358 8999 - 36 units - $130.

3-Star
Madison's Hotel, 6 Ward Avenue, ph 9357 1155 - 8 suites, 30 units - B&LtB $79.
Medina Executive Apartments, 68 Roslyn Gardens, ph 9356 7400 - 58 units - $85.
Roslyn Gardens Motor Inn, 4 Roslyn Gardens, ph 9358 1944 - 29 units - $59-79.

Glebe (3km west of the city)
3-Star
The Haven Inn Sydney, 196 Glebe Point Road, ph 9660 6655 - 51 units, licensed restaurant, heated swimming pool, spa - $99-119.
University Motor Inn, 25 Arundel Street, ph 9660 5777 - 45

units, licensed restaurant - $96.

Rooftop Motel, 146 Glebe Point Road, ph 9660 7777 - 39 units, swimming pool - $75-85.

2-Star

Hereford Lodge, 51 Hereford Street, ph 9660 5577 - 12 units, licensed bistro, swimming pool - $70.

Kings Cross (2km east of the city)

5-Star

Hyatt Regency Sydney, Top of William Street, ph 9356 1234 - 390 rooms, licensed restaurants, swimming pool - $165.

4-Star

The Crescent on Bayswater, 33 Bayswater Road, ph 9357 7266 - 46 suites, 24 rooms, **Studebaker's Nightclub**, brasserie and bar, swimming pool, fitness centre - $145-165.

Top of the Town Motel, 227 Victoria Street, ph 9361 0911 - 101 units, licensed restaurant, swimming pool - $150-175.

Hotel Capital, 111 Darlinghurst Road, ph 9358 2755 - 214 rooms, licensed restaurant, cocktail bar, swimming pool, spa, sauna, gym - $110.

Kingsview Motel, 30 Darlinghurst Road, ph 9358 5599 - 67 units, unlicensed restaurant - $68-105.

3-Star

Hampton Court Hotel, 9 Bayswater Road, ph 9357 2711 - 28 suites, 126 rooms - $90.

Metro Motor Inn, 40 Bayswater Road, ph 9356 3511 - 37 units - $75.

Lane Cove (9km north of the city)

4-Star

Metro Inn Apartments, 302 Burns Bay Road, ph 9427 4000 - 28 units, riverside location, heated swimming pool, squash - $129-149.

Country Comfort Motel, cnr Pacific Highway & Gatacre Ave, ph 9427 0266 - 43 units, unlicensed restaurant - $88.

North Sydney (4km north of the city)

4-Star

Rydges North Sydney, 54 McLaren Street, ph 9922 1311 - 48 suites, 167 rooms, licensed restaurant, cocktail bar - $120-165.

3-Star

Centra North Sydney Motel, Blue Street, ph 9955 0499 - 2 suites, 210 units, licensed restaurant, swimming pool - $155-250.

Potts Point (3km east of the city)

5-Star

The Landmark Parkroyal Sydney Hotel, 81 Macleay Street, ph 9368 3000 - 12 suites, 470 rooms, licensed restaurant, cocktail lounge, swimming pool - $170-280.

4-Star

Chateau Sydney Motel, 14 Macleay Street, ph 9358 2500 - 2 suites, 94 units, licensed restaurant, cocktail lounge, heated swimming pool - $120-140.

3-Star

The Dorchester Inn, 38 Macleay Street, ph 9358 2400 - 14 units - $90-140.
Sheraton Motor Hotel, 40 Macleay Street, ph 9358 1955 - 18 suites, 46 units, licensed restaurant, cocktail bar - $95.

Randwick (6km east of the city)

4-Star

Medina Apartments, 63 St Marks Road, ph 9399 5144 - 60 units, swimming pool, spa, sauna - $140-160 (for up to four people).
Gemini Motel, 65 Belmore Road, ph 9399 9011 - 97 units, licensed restaurant - $89.

3-Star

Esron Motel, cnr Dudley & St Pauls Streets, ph 9398 7022 - 41 units, swimming pool - $55-68.

2-Star

Royal Hotel, Cuthill Street, ph 9399 3006 - 19 rooms (1 with private facilities), licensed restaurant - $55-65. (A popular pub with uni students - could be noisy Thurs-Sat.)

Rushcutters Bay (3km east of the city)

3-Star

The Bayside Hotel, 85 New South Head Road, ph 9327 8511 - 99 rooms, licensed restaurants, cocktail lounge - B&B $99-155.

St Leonards (6km north of the city)

4-Star

Mercure Hotel, 194 Pacific Highway, ph 9439 6000 - 1 suite, 67 units, licensed restaurant, swimming pool - $99-188.
Greenwich Inn, 196 Pacific Highway, ph 9906 3277 - 25 units, licensed restaurant - $79-99.

Getting Around

Sydney has an efficient public transport system, with buses, ferries and trains covering the city and the suburban areas. For information on all public transport contact the Infoline, ph 13 15 00, 6am-10pm, 7 days.

Train

The main station is **Central (Railway Square).** All country trains begin their journey from here. All suburban trains pass through Central and Town Hall stations, and you can change at either to link up with the City Circle; to cross over the Harbour Bridge; or to board the train for Bondi Junction, which passes through Martin Place, Kings Cross and Edgecliff.

Central Station can be entered from Eddy Avenue, Elizabeth Street (best for suburban trains), or from the entrance road that runs off Pitt Street (best for country trains) to the left after crossing Hay Street if you are coming by car.

The stations in the City are:
Town Hall, Wynyard, Circular Quay, St James, Museum and Martin Place. These stations are all part of the underground network. The first five form the City Circle.
Wynyard Station has three entrances - one in George Street and two in York Street (one accessed from the transport interchange in Wynyard Park).
Town Hall Station has two entrances on each side of George Street. *St James Station* has entrances in Elizabeth Street and Queens Square.
Museum Station has entrances on both sides of Liverpool Street and one in Elizabeth Street.
Martin Place Station is well sign-posted, as is *Circular Quay Station.*

Tickets are purchased from a sales window before

commencement of a journey, or you can use one of the machines on the city stations.

Bus

Details of the routes and schedules of Sydney Buses can be found in the A-K Yellow Pages of the telephone book.

Generally speaking, buses from the Eastern Suburbs terminate at either Central Railway or Circular Quay; those from the North-western and Western Suburbs terminate at York Street (near the Queen Victoria Building) or Circular Quay; and North Shore and Northern Suburbs bus routes end at Wynyard Park, near Wynyard Station, or outside the Queen Victoria Building.

The Sydney Explorer Bus

The red Sydney Explorer bus is a great way to get around the city. It travels a 20km circuit to 20 different stops from 9.30am-9pm, every day except Christmas Day. Passengers can get on and off anywhere along the route, stay as long as they like at any stop, then catch the next Explorer to the next stop. If you miss the last Explorer bus, don't worry because your ticket is good on any State Transit bus within the Explorer route until midnight. The Explorer stops are:

1. Sydney Cove (Circular Quay)
2. Sydney Opera House
3. Royal Botanic Gardens
4. Mrs Macquarie's Chair
5. Art Gallery of NSW
6. Kings Cross
7. Elizabeth Bay House
8. Potts Point
9. The Australian Museum
10. Central Railway Station
11. Chinatown
12. Powerhouse Museum
13. Maritime Museum
14. Darling Harbour
15. Aquarium

16. Harbour Bridge
17. Milsons Point
18. Wynyard Park
19. Queen Victoria Building
20. The Rocks

Tickets can be purchased when boarding the bus, or beforehand from the NSW Travel Centre, 19 Castlereagh Street; Australian Pacific Tours, Shop 4, Overseas Shipping Terminal, Circular Quay West; CountryLink Rail Travel Centres; Sydney Tower, Centrepoint; or from a local travel agent. The fares for all day travel are **$20 adult, $15 child, $45 family** (2 adults and any number of children from the same family).

Bondi & Bay Explorer

Blue and white buses clearly marked Bondi & Bay Explorer operate on a circular route from the city centre to the eastern suburbs every thirty minutes, stopping at the following:

1. Circular Quay
2. Kings Cross
3. Rushcutters Bay
4. Double Bay
5. Rose Bay
6. Double Bay
7. Vaucluse Bay
8. Watsons Bay
9. The Gap park
10. Bondi Beach
11. Clovelly Beach
12. Coogee Beach
13. Randwick Racecourse
14. Sydney Cricket Ground
15. Paddington
16. Oxford Street
17. Hyde Park
18. Martin Place

Fares are the same as for the Sydney Explorer.

The public bus system is supplemented by various local private bus companies, which usually connect outlying places to the closest railway station. Some companies and

their areas are:
Busways - Blacktown - ph 9625 8900
Shorelink - North Shore - ph 9457 8888
Southtrans - Hurstville, Miranda, Sutherland -
ph 9543 4255
Westbus - Parramatta, Penrith - ph 9890 0000.

Ferry

Undoubtedly the most scenic way to travel, Sydney's ferries and rivercats ply between Circular Quay and Watsons Bay, Rose Bay, Manly, Taronga Zoo, Cremorne, Mosman, Neutral Bay, Kirribilli, Hunters Hill, Meadowbank, Parramatta, Birkenhead Point, Balmain and Darling Harbour. Full information on routes and schedules can also be found in the A-K Yellow Pages of the telephone directory.

Tickets for ferry travel are purchased at the ticket machines on the various wharves at the Circular Quay Ferry Terminal, either at the beginning or at the end of your trip. There are also change machines, so you don't have to worry about having the correct fare. You then use the ticket to open the exit gates.

Sydney Ferries also operate cruises that leave from Circular Quay. The 2½ hour River Cruise leaves at 10am daily ($16 adult, $12 child); the 2½ hour Harbour Cruise leaves at 10am daily ($16 adult, $12 child); and the 1½ hour Harbour Lights Cruise leaves at 8pm Mon-Sat ($14 adult, $10 child).

Tickets for the cruises can be purchased at the Ticket Office situated opposite the ferry wharves, near the entrance to Circular Quay Railway Station.

Special Fares

There are **several discount fares on offer,** and if you are going to be in the city for at least a week, it will pay you to invest in one of the TravelPasses. They are available for "Train-Bus-Ferry", "Bus-Ferry", "Train-Bus" and "Bus Only". They come in a variety of colours according to the methods of transport covered and the distances involved. Prices range from $20 to $45 for seven days, irrespective of how many trips are taken. Passes are available from most newsagents, and from transport offices, ph 13 15 00 for addresses.

CityHopper tickets are available and allow unlimited, one-day rail and bus travel around the City Circle. The ticket also includes Redfern, Milsons Point, North Sydney, Martin Place and Kings Cross stations. The ticket costs $5.00 adults, $2.50 children under 16, and is a very economical way of getting to the various city sights.

Another option is **TravelTen,** which can be used on buses only. This ticket comes in five different colours, representing the length of the trip it covers, and must be inserted in the green machine on entering the bus. It offers a saving of around 45% of the normal fare.

Then there is the **BusTripper,** an all-day ticket that allows travel on as many buses as you like in one day, but it really pays to make a long trip with this ticket as the further you go, the more you save. The cost of BusTripper is $7.80 adult, $3.90 child.

The **SydneyPass** provides unlimited bus and ferry travel, including Sydney Ferries harbour cruises, Explorer and Airport Express. Passes are available for:
3 days - $60 adult, $50 child
5 days - $80 adult, $70 child
7 days - $90 adult, $80 child.

The **Day Pass** is valid for unlimited travel on all bus and ferry services (except the tourist services) and costs $12 adult, $6 child.

The **Day Rover** is valid for unlimited travel on all bus and ferry (not the special tourist services) and CityRail trains in the Sydney metropolitan area. Costs are $20 adult, $10 child.

The Monorail

The monorail system runs anti-clockwise and has six stations - Harbourside (Darling Harbour), Convention Centre (Darling Harbour), Haymarket (Chinatown), World Square (Liverpool Street), Park Plaza (Pitt Street, near Park Street) and City Centre (Pitt Street, near Market Street). It is the best way to get from the city centre to Darling Harbour, and if you are travelling to the city by car, you can sometimes find cheap parking in Pyrmont behind the Darling Harbour complex, then take the monorail into the city.

The fare for the monorail is $2.50 for adults, $1.50 children, whether you are going one stop or the complete circuit. You are not permitted to stay aboard for more than one circuit. The system operates daily - Mon-Wed 7am-10pm, Thurs-Sat 7am-midnight, Sun 8am-9pm.

Sydney Light Rail

A tram system runs from Central Railway past Paddy's Market, Darling Harbour, Sydney Casino, the Fish markets and terminates at Wentworth Park greyhound racing track. It runs 24 hours a day and generally at 10 minute intervals. There are two zones for fares - Zone 1 (Central to Darling Harbour), Zone 2 (Darling Harbour to Wentwork Park). Fares per person are $2.00 one way, $3.00 return within a zone; $3.00 one way, $4.00 return travel over the two zones. Children are half fare. For further information phone 9660-5288.

Taxi

Sydney is well served by taxis and charges are set by the Department of Transport. The main cab companies are:
Taxis Combined Services, ph 9332 8888;
RSL Cabs, ph 9581 1111;
Legion Cabs, ph 13 1451;
Premier Cabs, ph 13 1017;
Specially outfitted cabs for people in wheelchairs are available, ph 1800 043 187. It is really best to booked these in advance.

CityRail Suburban Ne

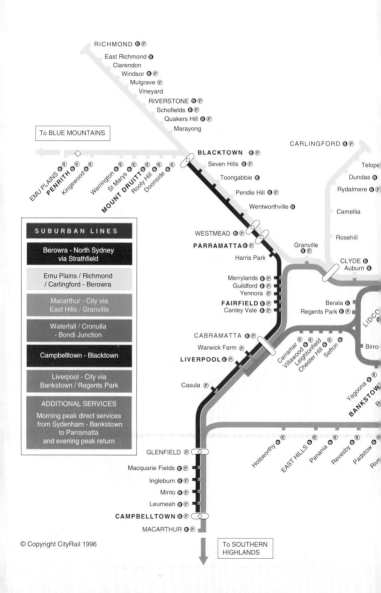

RICHMOND 🅑🅟
East Richmond 🅑
Clarendon
Windsor 🅑🅟
Mulgrave 🅟
Vineyard
RIVERSTONE 🅑🅟
Schofields 🅑🅟
Quakers Hill 🅑🅟
Marayong

CARLINGFORD 🅑🅟

To BLUE MOUNTAINS

BLACKTOWN 🅑🅟
Seven Hills 🅑🅟
Toongabbie 🅑
Pendle Hill 🅑🅟
Wentworthville 🅑

EMU PLAINS 🅑🅟 **PENRITH** 🅑🅟 Kingswood 🅑🅟 Werrington 🅑🅟 St Marys 🅑🅟 **MOUNT DRUITT** 🅑🅟 Rooty Hill 🅑🅟 Doonside 🅑🅟

Telope
Dundas 🅑
Rydalmere 🅑🅟

Camellia

WESTMEAD 🅑🅟
PARRAMATTA 🅑🅟
Harris Park

Granville
🅑🅟

Rosehill

CLYDE 🅑
Auburn 🅑

Merrylands 🅑🅟
Guildford 🅑🅟
Yennora 🅟
FAIRFIELD 🅑🅟
Canley Vale 🅑🅟

Berala 🅑
Regents Park 🅑🅟

LIDCC

CABRAMATTA 🅑🅟
Warwick Farm 🅟
LIVERPOOL 🅑🅟

Carramar 🅑🅟 Villawood 🅑🅟 Leightonfield 🅑 Chester Hill 🅑 Sefton 🅑

Birro

Casula 🅟

Yagoona 🅑🅟
BANKSTOW

SUBURBAN LINES

Berowra - North Sydney
via Strathfield

Emu Plains / Richmond
/ Carlingford - Berowra

Macarthur - City via
East Hills / Granville

Waterfall / Cronulla
- Bondi Junction

Campbelltown - Blacktown

Liverpool - City via
Bankstown / Regents Park

ADDITIONAL SERVICES
Morning peak direct services
from Sydenham - Bankstown
to Parramatta
and evening peak return

Holsworthy 🅑🅟 EAST HILLS 🅑🅟 Panania 🅑🅟 Revesby 🅑🅟 Padstow 🅑 Riv

GLENFIELD 🅟
Macquarie Fields 🅑🅟
Ingleburn 🅑🅟
Minto 🅑🅟
Leumeah 🅑🅟
CAMPBELLTOWN 🅑🅟
MACARTHUR 🅑🅟

© Copyright CityRail 1996

To SOUTHERN
HIGHLANDS

Unlike many cities such as in New Zealand, taxis may be hailed in the street. You can also hire them at a taxi rank, or a pick-up can be arranged by phone for an extra fee. This service has vastly improved in recent years.

Taxi ranks in the city include Central Station, Circular Quay, Park Street opposite the Town Hall, and outside all the major hotels.

If you hire a taxi in the city to take you over the bridge, $2 will be added to the bill even though there is no toll for travel south to north. This extra is added because the taxi driver has to pay the toll to travel over the bridge to return to the city, and may not get a fare going that way.

Water Taxi

Companies that operate water taxis are: *Water Taxis Combined*, ph 9810 5010; *Harbour Taxi Boats*, ph 8555 1155; and *Circular Quay Water Taxis*, ph 9810 1410.

They will take you from any landing point to any landing point on the harbour, and also offer scenic cruises.

Car

Renting a car is relatively cheap if you are travelling in a group, but **driving in the city is not really recommended.** The one-way streets take a bit of getting used to, and parking is a problem. Street parking is extremely hard to find, and the parking station fees add a lot to the cost of your day out. For travelling in the suburbs and outlying areas, a car is definitely the way to go.

Here are a few names of rental companies and their reservation phone numbers:

Avis, ph 9353 9000;

Budget, ph 13 2727;

Hertz, ph 13 3039;

Airport Rent A Car, ph 9599 3000.

International and overseas drivers licences that are in English are accepted, and a deposit, or credit card details, are required before pick-up. Other car rental companies

(Overleaf) Dusk in the Botanic Gardens; (Facing) Darling Harbour by day and night.

> When hiring a car it is important to check out what you are actually getting for your money.
> Is the company offering unlimited kilometres?
> Is the insurance cover adequate?
> If you decide to drive interstate, can you drop the car off in another city, or do you have to drive back to Sydney?
> Is the car entitled to NRMA (National Roads and Motorists Association) road service?
> Ask for an all inclusive price so that you won't be hit with extra charges at the end of the rental period.

are found in the A-K Yellow Pages of the Telephone Directory.

Traffic in Sydney drives on the left, and the speed limit in built-up areas is 60km/h, although some councils have brought in 50km/h on secondary roads and 40km/h near schools during school hours.

In recent years, a number of **roundabouts** have been installed, and the rules that apply here are that traffic already on the roundabout has right-of-way. The general driving rule is that cars have to give way to traffic on their right, but cars at a T-intersection have no right-of-way.

The NRMA has reciprocal arrangements with overseas and interstate automobile associations.
The phone number for enquiries is 13 2132, and for road service, 13 1111.

Toll for Harbour Bridge and Tunnel
Both the Harbour Bridge (Bradfield Highway) and the Cahill Tunnel have a toll fee of $2 for southbound cars. It should be mentioned that the Tunnel is not an alternative to the Bridge. It is for traffic heading for the airport and the eastern suburbs, and the Bridge is for traffic to the city and the Western Distributor.

Eating Out

Sydney has a plethora of restaurants offering every type of cuisine imaginable. The harbour foreshores are liberally sprinkled with eating establishments, for there are not too many experiences that beat, or for that matter match, a leisurely brunch on a sunny weekend with the harbour and all its craft as a backdrop. Unfortunately, though, you often have to pay 'over the top' for this indulgence. With so much competition, you would expect that prices would have to be kept to a minimum, but there are apparently enough people to ensure that each restaurant is well-patronised, and indeed bookings are essential when a water view is offered.

Restaurants are classified as *'Licensed'* or *'BYO'*.
Licensed means that the establishment has a licence to sell alcohol; *BYO* means 'bring your own' wine, etc, because the restaurant does not have a liquor licence.

Some restaurants, although licensed, allow patrons to supply their own wine (not beer or spirits), which is usually less expensive than paying the mark-up on the wines that the restaurant is legally allowed to add. Then a *corkage fee* may be added which will be per bottle or per person, but the end result is usually still less expensive.

Alcohol can be purchased from the *bottle department* of a hotel, or from one of the many *bottle shops* that abound in every suburb.

It is reasonable to say that the price of a bottle of wine in one of these shops would be less than half the price of the same wine in a restaurant.

One of Sydney's best, and most expensive, restaurants is **Level 41**, Chifley Tower, Chifley Square, ph 9221 2500. The view is magnificent, but complements rather than dominates the food. The cuisine is Modern Australia, and the presentation is first class. *Level 41* is open for lunch

Mon-Fri and for dinner Mon-Sat 6-10.30pm.

Running a close second, though some might say that it is a dead heat, is *The Rockpool*, 107 George Street, The Rocks, ph 9252 1888. The cuisine here is also Modern Australian, the presentation is excellent, and the prices are commensurate. Open for lunch Mon-Fri, dinner Mon-Sat.

Both the above are licensed and accept all credit cards.

At the other end of the scale is a Sydney landmark that has been around a very long time - *Harry's Café de Wheels*, Cowper Wharf Roadway, Woolloomooloo. It is not a restaurant, not even a cafe, just a roadside stall, but everyone knows *Harry's*, and their real Aussie meat pies and peas, etc, handed to you on a paper serviette, are yummy! Eating a pie in this fashion is an art form which most Sydneysiders are born with, but when in Rome....!

As for everything between the above two extremes, following is a list of recommended restaurants, rated
Expensive (main course $20+),
Moderate (main course $15-$20)
Budget (main course under $15).
Not included here are the restaurants in the 5-star hotels as everyone knows that they exist, and are much the same the world over with regard to menus and prices.

Credit card abbreviations are:
Amex = American Express; BC = Bankcard; DC = Diners Club; MC = MasterCard; V = Visa.

City and The Rocks
Bilson's, Upper Level, Overseas Passenger Terminal, Circular Quay West, ph 9251 5600 - Licensed - good harbour views - French/Australian cuisine - **Expensive** - open Sun-Fri noon-3pm, nightly 7-10pm - Amex, BC, DC, MC, V.

Doyle's at The Quay, Lower Level, Overseas Passenger Terminal, Circular Quay West, ph 9252 3400 - Licensed - good harbour views, outside tables - Seafood - **Expensive** - open Mon-Sun 11.30am-2.45pm, Mon-Sat 5.30-9.30pm, Sun 5.30-9pm - BC, DC, MC, V.

Bennelong, Sydney Opera House, Circular Quay, ph 9250 7578 - Licensed - good harbour views - Modern Australian cuisine (basically that means a bit of everything) - **Expensive** - open Mon-Sat pre-theatre from 6pm, dinner from 7pm, after-theatre from 10pm - Amex, BC, DC, MC, V.

MCA Cafe, Museum of Contemporary Art, Quayside, Circular Quay, ph 9241 4253 - Licensed - good harbour views, outdoor tables - Mediterranean-type cuisine - **Moderate** - open Mon-Fri 11am-5.30pm, Sun 9am-5.30pm - Amex, BC, MC, V.

Imperial Harbourside, 15 Circular Quay West, The Rocks, ph 9247 7073 - Licensed - good views, outdoor tables - Chinese cuisine - **Moderate** - open daily noon-3pm, Sun-Thurs 6-11pm, Fri-Sat 6pm-midnight - Amex, BC, DC, MC, V.

Phillip's Foote, 101 George Street, The Rocks, ph 9241 1485 - Licensed (it is actually a pub) - cook-your-own steaks, good salad bar, outdoor tables - **Budget** - open daily for lunch and dinner - Amex, BC, DC, MC, V.

Restaurant CBD, CBD Hotel, 75 York Street (cnr King Street), ph 9299 8911 - Licensed - British/Modern Australian - **Moderate** - open for lunch and dinner Mon-Fri - Amex, BC, DC, MC, V.

Rossini Rosticceria, Shop W5, Circular Quay, ph 9247 8026 - Licensed - good views, outside tables - Italian, cafeteria style - **Budget** - open daily 7-10.30am, 11am-4pm, 5-10.30pm - no credit cards accepted.

Paragon Cafe, 1st Floor, Paragon Hotel, Circular Quay, ph 9241 3888 - Licensed - Modern cuisine - **Moderate** - open Mon-Fri noon-3pm, Mon-Sat 6.30-10pm - Amex, BC, MC, V.

Merrony's, 2 Albert Street, Circular Quay, ph 9247 9323 - Licensed - Australian/French - **Moderate** - open Mon-Fri noon-2.30pm, Mon-Sat 5.45-11.45pm, Sun 5.45-10pm - Amex, BC, DC, MC, V.

EJ's, 143 Macquarie Street, City (lower ground floor), ph 9247 8968 - Licensed - cuisine is a bit of everything from everywhere - **Moderate** - open for lunch only Mon-Fri noon-2.30pm - Amex, BC, DC, MC, V.

Claudine's on Macquarie, 151 Macquarie Street, City, ph 9241 1749 - Licensed & BYO - Seafood/French - **Moderate** - open Mon-Fri 7.30-11.30am, noon-3pm, 5.30-8.30pm - Amex, BC, DC, MC, V.

Botanic Gardens Restaurant, once in the Gardens, follow the signs, ph 9241 2419 - Licensed - good views - casual dining, outdoor tables - **Moderate** - open daily noon-2.15pm - Amex, BC, MC, V.

Dendy Bar & Bistro, 19 Martin Place, ph 9221 1243 - Licensed - extensive menu - **Budget** - open Mon-Sat noon-9.30pm, Sun noon-6pm - Amex, BC, MC, V.

Bridges, 4 Bridge Street, City, ph 9221 5862 - Licensed - Southern Mediterranean cuisine - **Moderate** - open Mon-Fri noon-2.30pm, 6-9pm - Amex, BC, DC, MC, V.

Zolie's Restaurant, 5 York Street, City, ph 9299 3276 - European cuisine - **Moderate** - open Mon-Fri noon-3pm, nightly 6-10pm - Amex, BC, DC, MC, V.

Papillon, 71 York Street, City, ph 9299 7292 - Licensed - French cuisine - **Expensive** - open Mon-Fri noon-3pm, Tues-Fri 6-9pm - Amex, BC, DC, MC, V.

Kamogawa, Corn Exchange Building, cnr Sussex & Market Streets, City, ph 9299 5533 - Licensed - Japanese, with teppan bar, traditional rooms and conventional dining area - **Moderate to Expensive,** depending on locale - open daily 6.30-10am, 6-10pm, Mon-Sat noon-3pm, karaoke bar Mon-Fri 8.30pm-1am - Amex, BC, DC, MC, V.

Choys Jin Jiang, 2nd floor, Queen Victoria Building, Sussex Street, City, ph 9261 3388 - Licensed - Chinese - **Moderate** - open daily noon-3pm, Sun-Mon 5.30-10pm, Tues-Thurs 5.30-11pm, Fri-Sat 5.30pm-midnight - Amex, BC, DC, MC, V.

Planet Hollywood, 600 George Street, ph 9267 7827 - the 32nd link in this world-wide chain of movie themed restaurants - Licensed - **Moderate** - open daily 11am-1am - does not take reservations.

Chinatown (Haymarket)

Golden Harbour, 31 Dixon Street, ph 9212 5987 - Licensed & BYO (corkage fee $4 per bottle) - Cantonese - **Budget** - open Mon-Fri 10am-4.30pm, 5.30-11pm, Sat-Sun 9am-4.30pm, 5.30pm-1am - Amex, BC, DC, MC, V.

House of Guang Zhou, 76 Ultimo Road, ph 9281 2205 - Licensed - Chinese - **Budget** - open Mon-Fri 11.30am-3pm, Sat-Sun noon-3pm, daily 5.30pm-2am - Amex, BC, DC, MC, V.

Marigold, Levels 4 & 5, 683-689 George Street, ph 9281 3388 - Licensed & BYO (corkage fee $1.50 per person) - Cantonese - **Moderate** - open daily 10am-3pm, 5.30pm-midnight - Amex, BC, DC, MC, V.

Bali Bagoes Indonesian Restaurant, 160 Thomas Street, Ultimo, ph 9281 3017 - Licensed & BYO (corkage fee $1 per bottle) - **Budget** - open daily 11am-11pm - Amex, BC, DC, MC, V.

Jing May Noodle, 1st floor, Prince Centre, 160 Thomas Street, Haymarket, ph 9281 2387 - BYO - Chinese - **Budget** - open Mon-Tues, Thurs-Sun 11am-11pm - no credit cards accepted.

Malaya, 761 George Street, ph 9211 0946 - Licensed - Malaysian cuisine - **Budget** - open daily noon-3pm, Mon-Sat 5-10pm, Sun 5-9pm - Amex, BC, DC, MC, V.

East Sydney

Beppi's, cnr Yurong & Stanley Streets, ph 9360 4558 - Licensed - Italian cuisine - **Expensive** - open Mon-Fri noon-3pm, Mon-Sat 6-11.30pm - Amex, BC, DC, MC, V.

Yutaka, 200 Crown Street, ph 9361 3818 - Licensed & BYO (corkage fee $1 per person) - Japanese cuisine - **Moderate** - open Mon-Fri noon-2.15pm, Mon-Sat 6-10.45pm, Sun 6-10pm - Amex, BC. MC, V.

Tre Scalini, 174 Liverpool Street, ph 9331 4358 - Licensed - Italian cuisine - **Expensive** - open Mon-Fri noon-2.30pm, Mon-Sat 6-10.30pm - Amex, BC, MC, V.

Ristorante Mario, 38 Yurong Street, ph 9331 4945 - Licensed - Italian cuisine - **Expensive** - open Mon-Fri noon-3pm, Mon-Sat 6.30-11pm - BC, MC, V.

No Names, 2 Chapel Street, ph 9360 4711 - BYO - Italian pasta and minestrone - **Budget** - open for lunch and dinner - no credit cards accepted. There are several *No Names* restaurants around Sydney, but this is the original, and most people think it is still the best.

Cruising Restaurants

Captain Cook Cruises, ph 9206 1111, have lunch and dinner options. The *Luncheon Cruise* departs Circular Quay at 12.30pm, lasts 1½ hours and includes a Buffet Luncheon featuring Sydney rock oysters, Tasmanian trout, rare roast beef, ham, chicken, fresh salads, fruit platters and Australian cheeses - **$42 adult, $32 child.**

The *Captain Cook Showtime Dinner Cruise* leaves from Wharf 6 Circular Quay at 7.30pm. The cruises on Tues, Wed, Thurs & Sun finish at 10pm, but on Fri and Sat they continue until 11.30pm, and offer dancing with the showtime band. **The cost is $79.** Reservations essential.

The John Cadman Cruising Restaurant cruises every night of the year and departs Wharf 6 Circular Quay at 7.30pm. It returns at 10pm and 11pm. The a la carte menu is prepared by international chefs, and there is a selection of Australian and imported wines. **Cost of the dinner cruise is $84,** and reservations are essential, ph 9206 1111.

Captain Cook Cruises also offer Coffee, Luncheon and Explorer Cruises.

Sail Venture Cruises have luncheon and dinner cruises on their Big Cats, with changing menus. The luncheon cruise departs Darling Harbour Aquarium Wharf at 12.15pm (returning at 2.25pm) and Campbells Cove, Circular Quay, at 12.35pm (returning at 2.05pm) - **$35 adult, $18 child.**

The dinner cruise departs Darling Harbour at 7pm (returning at 10.10pm) and Campbells Cove at 7.30pm (returning at 9.45pm) - **$48 adult, $25 children**.
For reservations and enquiries, ph 9262 3595.

Matilda Cruises serve lunch on their two-hour harbour cruises, which leave Darling Harbour Aquarium Wharf at 11.30am and 1.30pm, Campbells Cove Circular Quay at 11.45am and 1.45pm, and Taronga Zoo at 12.45pm and 2.45pm. **The cruises cost $22 adult, $12 children,** and an **Aussie Bar-B-Q lunch cooked on board costs an extra $8.50.** Reservations are necessary, ph 9264 7377.

Matilda Cruises also operate the *Solway Lass*, a tall ship, which has a luncheon sail departing daily from Darling Harbour Aquarium Wharf at 12.15pm (boarding at noon) and returning at 1.45pm - **$35 adults, $18 children.** The dinner cruise *Dine Under Canvas,* sails Fri and Sat, boarding at 6.30pm, sailing at 7pm, and returning at 10pm - carvery dinner, with fully stocked bar and wine cellar - **$45 adults.** Bookings are essential.

Bounty Cruises have lunch and dinner cruises aboard the tall ship *Bounty,* and they always guarantee that part of the cruise will be under sail. The cruises leave from Campbells Cove Wharf, where you can also inspect the *Bounty,* which is a replica of the one that Captain Bligh sailed on and was built for the movie *Mutiny on The Bounty.* The lunch cruise departs on Sat, Sun and public holidays at 12.30pm, and the dinner cruise on Fri and Sat (and Sun of a long weekend) at 7pm. Both cruises offer **buffet-style meals and cost $45 adult,** with 50% discount for children 5-15.Children under 5 years sail free. For reservations, ph 9247 1789.

Don't think for one moment that the above lists all the restaurants in Sydney. It is little more than the tip of the iceberg. Often you will find restaurants in the same street as the one listed here, which we have not included. The above does, however, give you somewhere to start.

On weekends, it is a wise idea to phone ahead and book a table.

In case you are wondering about the availability of a Big Mac, be reassured that there are 14 *McDonald's* in the city. *Pizza Hut* has two city branches; and *KFC* has one in the city, and one at Darling Harbour.

Entertainment

As mentioned in the Introduction chapter, the Friday edition of *The Sydney Morning Herald* has "Metro", and the Thursday edition of the *Daily Telegraph* has *7 Days* which list what's on at all of Sydney's night spots.

It would be lengthy and boring to list all the venues in the city and suburbs, so we took a survey amongst a group of Sydney ragers and the following are their favourites.

Night Clubs

City

Harbourside Brasserie, Pier One, Millers Point,
ph 9252 3000. It has two cocktail bars and commands sweeping views of Sydney Harbour.

Hours:	Mon-Fri 6pm-2am, Sat 6pm-4am, Sun 6pm-10pm, dinner to 11pm (may be closed on Monday in the middle of winter).
Live Entertainment:	6 nights.
Cover charge:	$7-$20 depending on act.
Dinner and show:	$45 depending on act.
Comment:	very popular, not bad.

Paragon Hotel, cnr Loftus & Alfred Streets, ph 9241 3522.

Hours:	Fri-Sat, noon-5am (restaurant only open for lunch Mon-Fri).
Cover charge:	Sat $15 after 9pm.
Age Group:	Fri - business crowd; later - 18 years+; Sat - 18-30 years.
Comment:	popular.

Orient Hotel, cnr Argyle & George Streets, ph 9251 1255.

Hours:	7 days 10.00am-3am (live bands every night of the week).
Cover charge:	free entry.
Age Group:	20-30 years.

Nightclub and live bands set out over three floors. Plenty of space.

Comment:	Tourist spot, very popular.

Retro Bar, Basement, CML Building Cnr Pitt Street & Martin Place, City, Tel: 9223 2220, Internet Address: Http//www.clubretro.com.au

Opening Hours:	Thursday to Saturday: 6 pm – 5 am, Open for Private Functions Sunday to Wednesday
Happy Hours:	None
Clientele:	Mainstream 21 – 45
Floorshows:	International/Local Acts; Customers
Music:	Live Bands (Retro/Cover); Retro
Dress Standards:	Neat & Tidy
Food Available:	Restaurant 6 pm to 12 am; light menu till 3.00 am
Cover Charge:	$10 Fri/Sat; Free on Thursday
Comment:	popular.

Riche, Hilton International Hotel, 259 Pitt Street, ph 9266 0610.

Hours:	Wed 9pm-late, Fri-Sat 9pm-late.
Cover Charge:	Wed - Fantastic Voyage theme - $10. Fri $15, Sat $10 after 10pm.
Age Group:	25 - 30 years.
Comment:	older crowd, good.

Bar Luna, Jackson's on George, 176 George Street, ph 9247 2605. The Club is upstairs, the restaurant is downstairs.

Hours:	Tues-Sat, 10pm-5am (restaurant service ceases 9.30pm).
Cover charge:	$6 after 10pm, Fri-Sat.
Age Group:	20-30 years.
Comment:	Very popular and the beer flows freely here.

Riva, Sheraton On The Park, 130 Castlereagh Street, City, Tel: 9286 6666

Opening Hours:	10 pm to late Wednesday to Saturday
Happy Hours:	None

Clientele:	Mixed 18 - 40
	Wednesday is Hospitality Night
Floorshows:	R&B Live Bands; Dance Acts; Fashion
	Parades – all on various nights
Music:	High Energy Dance in room one
	R&B/Funk in room two
Dress Standards	Smart – no jeans Friday/Saturday;
	no sandshoes anytime.
Food Available:	Light Snacks ie fries and wedges.
Cover Charge:	$12 Wednesday to Friday; $18 Saturday
Comment:	Excellent atmosphere.

Darling Harbour/Pyrmont

The Cave at Star City, Pirrama Road, Pyrmont, ph 9566 4755.

Opening Hours:	9.00pm to late (24 hour licence)
	7 days a week.
Happy Hours:	None
Clientele:	21-35 upmarket
Floorshows:	International/local acts, Live Bands;
	Cabaret Acts, local & international DJs.
Music:	House; R&B; Soul, mixture.
	Best to phone.
Dress Standards:	Smart Casual, No sandshoes, no jeans.
Food Available:	light menu, licenced.
Cover Charge:	$5-$20 depending on night,
	Saturday nigt $20.
Comment:	None

Sydney Show Boat, 235 Pyrmont Street (office), ph 9552 2722.

Hours:	Nightly Dinner Cruise 7.30-10pm -
	a la carte 3 course - $108 per person.
	Showtime 8.50-9.50pm.
	Lunch Cruise 12.30-2pm -
	Buffet meal plus Dixieland Jazz band
	and comedy magician - $48 per person.
	Sightseeing cruises 10.30am, 2.30pm &
	5.30pm - 1¼ hours - $18 per person.
Age Group:	25+ years.

Kings Cross

Orb, cnr Craigend & Victoria Streets, Darlinghurst, ph: 9360 3571

Opening Hours:	6pm – 3 am Friday & Saturday
Happy Hours	None
Clientele	18 – 35
Floorshows	From October – Live Bands
Music	House, Funk, Soul
Food Available	Restaurant 6 pm to 11 pm
Cover Charge	$10/15
Comment:	popular.

Round Midnight, 2 Roslyn Street, ph 9356 4045.

Hours:	Wed-Sun 6pm-6am.
Cover charge:	$5-10.

Offers jazz, soul and reggae. Dress is smart/casual.

Age Group:	25+ years.
Comment:	popular.

Sugareef, 20 Bayswater Road, Kings Cross, ph 9368 0763

Opening Hours	8 pm to late Tuesday to Sunday. Closed Monday
Happy Hours	None
Clientele	18-35
Floorshows	None
Music	Modern Dance, Mixed
Dress Standards	Smart/Dressy
Food Available	Snacks – light pizzas
Cover Charge	$10-15
Comment:	Popular

Darlinghurst

Kinselas, 383 Bourke Street, Darlinghurst, ph 9331 2699

Opening Hours	Wednesday to Sunday 8 pm – 3am; Sunday closes at 12 am Friday opens at 6 pm.
Happy Hours:	Friday 6 pm to 8 pm ($3.50 approx. for mixed drinks)
Clientele:	Various: 18 – 35/40; Girls Night on

	top floor on Sundays
Floorshows:	Friday Night Live Bands on top floor

This building was once Kinsela's Funeral Parlour.

Comment:	You can find better.

The Cauldron, 207 Darlinghurst Road, ph 9331 1523.
Very popular venue with the smart, well-dressed crowd,
bookings advised.

Hours:	Tues-Sat 6pm-3am.
Cover Charge:	$10.
Age Group:	25-35 years.
Comment:	very popular.

North Shore
Greenwood Hotel, 36 Blue Street, North Sydney, ph:
9964 9477

Opening Hours:	Monday to Saturday: 11 am to late
Happy Hours:	None
Clientele:	Thursday: 18 – 24
	Friday: Business; Mixed
Floorshows:	Periodical Acts
Music:	Jazz Quartet on Fridays 5 pm – 9pm
	Modern Dance on Thursday Night
	New Age/Cutting Edge Dance
	on Friday/Saturday
Dress Standards:	Neat Casual; Smart Casual on Friday
	No thongs, no tank tops
Food Available:	Restaurant open 11 am to 10 pm 6 days;
	6.30 pm to 10 pm on Saturday
	Turkish Bread outside above hours
Cover Charge:	Nil
Comment:	A very good club/bar; nice atmosphere.

Metropole Hotel, 287 Military Road, Cremorne, ph 9909
8888

Opening Hours:	10 pm until 5 am (ish) Friday/
	Saturday only
Happy Hours:	None
Clientele:	Upmarket 20 – 35
Floorshows:	None
Music:	Live Bands in Bar areas and

	occasionally in Club; Top 40,
	Acid Funk/House
Dress Standards:	Smart Casual
Food Available:	Light Snacks until Midnight; gourmet
	pizzas till dawn
Cover Charge	Friday only $5
Comment:	Very upmarket and popular.

Paddington

Fringe Bar, 106 Oxford Street, Paddington, ph 9360 3554

Opening Hours:	11.30 am to 12 am Monday to Thursday
	Sunday, 11.30 am to 3 am Friday
	to Saturday
Happy Hours:	None
Clientele:	Varies, 18 – 25 or 21 – 30 depending on
	night of the week
Floorshows:	Comedy Act on Monday Nights
Music:	Disco, Funk, Jazz, Acid Jazz
Dress Standards:	Smart Casual
Food Available:	Restaurant – pasta/pizza
Cover Charge:	Monday Comedy Act $3;
	no charge other nights

Bars & Bistros

City

Bridie O'Reilly's, corner Kent and Erskine Streets, ph 9279 3133.

Hours:	11am-midnight (Mon-Thurs),
	11am-2am (Fri-Sat), 11am-10pm (Sun).
	Bistro
Live Entertainment:	Irish bands, light entertainment.
Cover Charge:	None
Age Group:	25+ years

Bridie O'Reilly's, cnr George and Hay Streets, ph 9212 2111.

Hours:	11am-midnight (Mon-Thurs),
	11am-2am (Fri-Sat), 11am-10pm (Sun).

(Facing) Coffee at Bondi Beach; (Overleaf) One view of the Queen Victoria Building shopping complex.

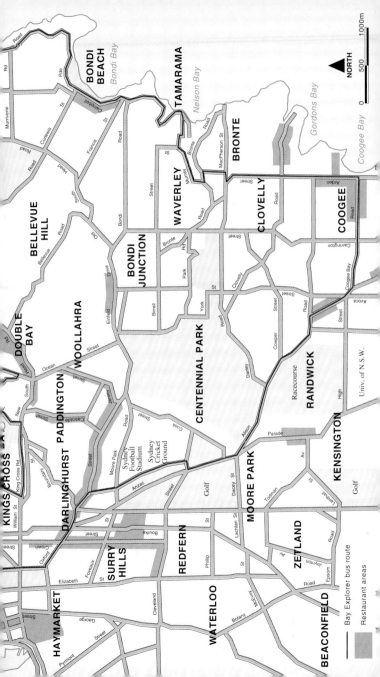

Bistro
Live Entertainment: Irish bands, light entertainment.
Cover Charge: None
Age Group: 25+ years

Horizons Bar, ANA Hotel, 176 Cumberland Street,
The Rocks, ph 9250 6000.
Hours: noon-1am (Mon-Sat) noon-11pm (Sun).
                     Light lunch noon-2pm.
Age Group: Older age group
Great harbour views.

Lucy's Tavern, 54 Castlereagh Street, ph 9221 3908.
Hours: Mon-Thurs 10.30am-10pm,
                     Fri-Sat 10.30am-5am.
Happy Hour: Mon-Fri 4pm-6pm & Sat 6pm-9pm.
Live Entertainment: Strip floorshow Wednesday 7.30pm,
                     occasional live bands on Saturday.
Cover charge: Free entry.
Age group: 18-30 years.
Comment: Pretty gross but its popular.

Marble Bar, Hilton Hotel, Pitt Street, ph 9266 0610.
The Marble Bar was part of the Adams Hotel, dating from
1893, which was built by George Adams, founder of Tatts
Lotto. When the Hotel was being refurbished by the new
owners, the Italian Renaissance Marble Bar was
dismantled stone by stone and rebuilt on the completion
of the Hotel that stands today.
Hours: Mon-Wed noon-11pm,
                     Thurs noon-midnight,
                     Fri noon-2am, Sat 3pm-2am,
                     Sun 5-11pm.
Happy Hour: Mon-Sat 5pm-7pm,
Cocktail Happy
Hour: Mon-Sat 7-9pm.
Live Entertainment: Wed-Sun.
Cover charge: Only for an unusually big name act.
Age group: 18-55 years.
Comment: Dressy and posh.

Arizona, 150 Day Street, ph 9261 4444.
Set with a Western theme. The floor is scattered with the discarded shells of peanuts, that are located around the bar in barrels to eat at your leisure. The bar runs various interesting competitions.

Hours:	Mon-Fri noon-11pm, lunch and dinner.
	Sat-Sun 4pm-11pm.
Happy Hour	5pm-7pm.
Cover charge:	Free entry.
Live entertainment:	Thurs-Sat.
Age Group:	25-40 years (not a young crowd).

Customs House, Sydney Renaissance Hotel, 30 Pitt Street, ph 9259 7000.
The bar is at the rear of the hotel and opens onto Macquarie Place Park where, in summer, a crowd of business movers and shakers spend their evenings. In operation since 1846, it has been said that should a bomb explode in this bar on any Friday evening, the Australian Stock Exchange would not open come Monday morning, not to mention the banking, legal and accounting professions.

Hours:	Mon-Fri 11am-10pm (closed weekends).
	Lunch is served from noon-2pm, there
	is no dinner service.
Happy Hour:	4.30-5.30pm.
Age Group:	21-35 years.

Woolloomooloo Bay Hotel, 2 Bourke Street, ph 9357 1177.
The Woolloomooloo is a great place to spend a Sunday afternoon in summer. The patrons spill onto the pavement outside whilst the band is playing.

Hours:	Mon-Sat 10am-11pm, Sun 11pm-9pm,
	bistro lunch and dinner 12pm-9pm.
Live entertainment:	Fri: 7.30-11pm - live music.
	Sat: 7:30-11pm - piano bar.
	Sun: 5:30-9pm - live music.
Cover charge:	Free entry.

Darling Harbour
Craig Brewery Bar & Grill, Festival Market Place, Darling Harbour, ph 9281 3922.

Hours:	Mon-Wed 10am-noon,
	Thurs-Sat 10am-3am.
	Dinner - cook your own steaks on the barbecue.
Happy Hour:	Mon-Fri 5:30-8:00pm.
Nightclub:	8pm-late.
Cover charge:	Fri-Sat $10 after 9pm.
Age Group:	18-35 years.

Pumphouse Tavern Brewery, 17 Little Pier Street, Darling Harbour, ph 9281 3967.

Hours:	Mon-Fri 11am-late, dinner till 9pm, nightclub and live bands.
Cover charge:	Free entry.
Age Group:	18-30 years.

The pumphouse is known for the fabulous boutique beers available on tap.

East of the city

Kings Cross
Bourbon & Beefsteak, 24 Darlinghurst Road, Kings Cross, ph 9358 1144.
The Bourbon and Beefsteak is an institution. Nearly every Sydneysider has visited the Bourbon at least once.

Hours:	24 hours, 7 days a week, dinner 7.30-10.30pm
Happy Hour:	every day 4-7pm.
Pianist:	4:30-9pm.
Jazz:	9pm-midnight.
Rock & Roll:	9pm-midnight.
Disco:	Fri-Sat 10pm-6am.
Cover charge:	Fri-Sat after 11pm.
Age Group:	All ages.

Darlinghurst
Burdekin Hotel, 2 Oxford Street, ph 9331 3066.

| *Hours*: | 11am-2pm, lunch & dinner |
| | 7.30-10.30pm. |

Paddington

London Tavern, 85 Underwood Street, ph 9331 6192 (restaurant), 9331 1637 (bar), 9331 3213 (office).
Pool Tables and card machines available.

Hours:	Mon-Thurs 11am-11pm,
	Fri-Sat 10am-11:15pm.
Happy Hour:	6:30-7:30pm; Thurs Beer Bust -
	cheaper beer, Dinner 6pm-10pm.
Age Group:	all ages.

Pubs

New Government regulations have now allowed pubs to have poker machines. This has led to the assertion that the State of New South Wales has 10% of the world's poker machines. When you take into account the existence of las vegas this is saying something.

City

Lord Nelson Brewery Hotel, 19 Kent Street, ph 9251 4044.

| *Hours*: | Mon-Sat 11am-11pm, Sun noon-10pm. |

The Lord Nelson claims to be the oldest continually licensed hotel, and the only pub brewery in Sydney brewing natural ales.

Mercantile Hotel, 25 George Street, The Rocks, ph 9247 3570.

Hours:	Mon-Thurs 10am-midnight,
	Fri-Sat 10am-1am.
Live Entertainment:	Every night except Tuesday; Sat and
	Sun afternoon.

The Mercantile is frequented by Irish travellers and is known as the Irish Pub. It has an Irish flavour and St Patrick's Day, March 17 is a big day for the Mercantile. They even serve green beer!

The Hero of Waterloo Hotel, 81 Lower Fort Street, ph 9252 4553.

Hours:	Mon-Sat 10am-11pm, Sun 10am-10pm. Bistro lunches and dinners available seven days.
Live Entertainment:	Fri, Sat and Sun nights, and old time music on Sat and Sun afternoons.

Museum downstairs shows a tunnel which runs down to the harbour. This pub is the oldest continuously trading pub in Sydney. Built in 1843.

Jazz Venues

The Basement, 29 Reiby Place, City, ph 9251 2797.

Hours:	open nightly for dinner, Mon-Fri for lunch.
Happy Hour:	Mon-Fri 4.30-6.30pm.
Cover charge:	depends on the artist.
Age Group:	25-55.

Features modern local and international artists and serves contemporary Australian food.

Comment: Excellent music and food. Guaranteed to have a good time. For Jazz lovers.

Soup Plus, 383 George Street, City, ph 9299 7728.

Hours:	Mon-Fri noon-midnight, Jazz 7:30-midnight; Sat-Sun noon-2am Jazz 8pm-12.30am.
Cover charge	and 2-course meal: $20 (Fri-Sat). 3-course meal: $23 (Fri-Sat). Mon-Fri - cover charge and $5-7 for entrees, $10-12 for mains.

Comment: good.

Strawberry Hills Hotel, 453 Elizabeth Street, Surry Hills, ph 9698 2997.

Hours:	Mon-Thurs 11am-midnight, Fri-Sat 11am-12.30am, Sun noon-10.30pm.
Restaurant	noon-3pm, 6-9.30pm.
Contemporary Jazz	Tues-Wed 8.30-11.30pm - $6-10.

Thursday-	Jazz 8.30-11.30pm - around $5.
Friday -	Jazz 7pm-12.30am (no cover charge).
Saturday -	Jazz 8pm-12.30am (no cover charge).
Sunday -	Jazz from 3-6pm, 7-10.30pm
Cover Charge:	None

Comment: good.

The Classics

The Sydney Opera House is **the** venue in Sydney for Opera, Ballet, and performances by the Sydney Symphony Orchestra.

The newly refurbished Sydney Town Hall is also the scene of musical evenings. The "Metro" has the information on programs, locations and times.

Theatres

Sydney has a vibrant theatre scene, and the local talent compares favourably with the rest of the world.

The large theatres have cocktail bars for pre-show or intermission drinks, and most of them have banned smoking in these areas, as well as in the auditoriums themselves. Some theatres have restaurants attached, where service is geared to getting patrons into the theatre on time.

Then there are the small theatre groups, and local dramatic and musical societies, whose performances are quite professional and you may see a star in the making for half the price required when he or she makes the big time. For example, **NIDA,** the National Institute of Dramatic Art (where Mel Gibson learnt his craft) presents plays at The Parade Theatre at 125 Anzac Parade, Kensington, ph 9697 7613, opposite the main entrance to the University of New South Wales. Prices vary according to the production but range from $17 to $20, not much more than you pay to see Mel in a movie.

Half-tix

Speaking of prices, Sydney has a **Half-tix booth** in Martin Place near Elizabeth Street, and it sells tickets to major venues at half price on the day of the performance.

It is open between noon and 6pm Monday to Saturday, and it's cash only, with no telephone bookings.

Major Theatres

Sydney Opera House has two theatres -the *Drama Theatre*, which seats 544, and the *Playhouse*, which seats 398. The Box Office is open Mon-Sat 9am-8.30pm, and charge telephone bookings may be made by phone, dial 9250 7777. There are several eateries at the Opera House itself, or you can choose from those in the area of Circular Quay.

Her Majesty's Theatre, 107 Quay Street, ph 9212 3411, is close to Central Railway Station and within walking distance of the restaurants of Chinatown.

Capitol Theatre, 17 Campbell Street, Haymarket, ph 9320 5000, recorded show information 1900 957 313. Recently renovated, the theatre is in Haymarket, near Chinatown.
The Theatre Royal, MLC Centre, King Street, ph 9231 6111, is in the heart of the city.

The Ensemble Theatre, 78 Mc Dougall Street, Milsons Point, ph 9929 8877, is situated in the Lower North Shore and has its own restaurant.

The Wharf Theatre, Pier 4, Hickson Road, Millers Point (The Rocks), ph 9250 1700, also has a restaurant, ph 9250 1761.

Belvoir Street Theatre, 25 Belvoir Street, Surry Hills, ph 9699 3444, doesn't have a restaurant, but does have a licensed bar offering light snacks before and after the show.

Seymour Theatre Centre, cnr Cleveland Street & City Road, Chippendale, ph 9692 3511, has three theatres - the *York*, *Everest* and *Downstairs*, and a very good restaurant, ph 9692 4138. There is also a coffee and snack bar in the upstairs foyer.

The Footbridge Theatre, Parramatta Road, Glebe, ph 9320 9000, is actually in the grounds of Sydney University. It doesn't have a restaurant of its own, but there are plenty nearby in Glebe.

Small Theatres

Stables Theatre, 10 Nimrod Street, Kings Cross, ph 9361 3817.
Kent Street Theatre, 420 Kent Street, City, ph 9529 9190.
Bay Street Theatre, 75 Bay Street, Glebe, ph 9692 0977.
New Theatre, 542 King Street, Newtown, ph 9519 6999.
Pilgrim Theatre, 262 Pitt Street, City, ph 9261 8981.
Enmore Theatre, 116 Enmore Road, Enmore, ph 9550 3666.

These small theatres may not have a current presentation when you are in town, and others not mentioned here may have something that you would be interested in seeing. Check "Metro" for details.

Rock Concerts

The main venue for these is the *Sydney Entertainment Centre,* near Chinatown.

If the person or group is a big star, eg Michael Jackson, Billy Joel & Elton John the promoters may opt to stage the concert at the Sydney Cricket Ground, even during the cricket season.

The Sydney Entertainment Centre is also used for ice shows, tennis tournaments, boxing matches, etc.

Cinemas

The main cinema area in the city is in George Street, between Park and Liverpool Streets.
Here is found:
Village Cinema Centre, 545 George Street, ph 9264 6701,

with 6 cinemas; *Hoyts Centre*, 505 George Street, ph 9267 9877, with 7 cinemas; *Greater Union*, 525 George Street, ph 9267 8666, with 4 cinemas.

Greater Union also has the *Pitt Centre*, 232 Pitt Street, ph 9264 1694, with another 3 cinemas.

Other cinemas in the city are:
Dendy in Martin Place, ph 9233 8166;
Mandolin, 150 Elizabeth Street, ph 9267 1968,
Encore Cinema, 64 Devonshire Street, ph 9281 1788.
As a general rule, Tuesday is half-price night at all cinemas, although some offer discounts on other nights.

Gambling Venues

The Sydney Harbour Casino, is close to Darling Harbour, and can be reached by ferry and bus. There are the usual assortment of blackjack tables, roulette tables, etc, and hundreds of poker machines (slot machines) were people queue up to lose their money.

At a cost of $867 million, the complex contains: a 352-room 5-star hotel, a lyric theatre seating 2000, a cabaret room seating 900, 14 restaurants, 12 bars, designer-name retail outlets, conference facilities, and 139 serviced apartments in the adjoining tower. It has its fair share of critics.

There are plenty of other places to go if you feel like a flutter. Firstly there are the **Clubs** - Leagues Clubs, RSL (Returned Servicemen's League) Clubs, Bowling Clubs, Worker's Clubs, Golf Clubs - which all have poker machines (that seem to offer better odds than those at the Casino), and most have keno.

Of course, it is not compulsory to play the pokies, and in fact, a lot of people don't, they go to the club to get a reasonably priced meal, and enjoy whatever entertainment is on offer. This varies from imported acts to cabaret shows with local talent, to movies, to chook raffles (yes, you do actually win a chook, or should I say a dead chicken).

Every suburb has one or more clubs, but if you are a first-time visitor to Sydney, I suggest that you stick to the suburban League Clubs. They are bigger, brighter, busier, and you can experience a good cross-section of Sydney life. Clubs are listed in the Yellow Pages of the Telephone Directory under *Clubs - Social and General.*

Although the clubs are there primarily for the use of members, **visitors are always made welcome,** as long as they are suitably dressed - no thongs, a collar with a shirt, and in the evening, long pants are preferred. Those dress rules are of course for men. Women must be 'decently' attired. Remember to sign the visitor's book in the foyer.

The clubs also have TAB (Totalisator Agency Board) facilities and SKY Channel television. This means that you can study the form guide in the comfort of a well-appointed club with a cold glass of whatever you fancy, place bets on your favourite horses, watch the race live, then collect your winnings (or tear up your ticket). Perhaps it should be mentioned that SKY Channel is only available to TAB agencies and licensed premises.

If you are not into the club scene you can, of course, place your bets at the local TAB agency, and they are in every suburb, but there is no atmosphere.

Alternatively you can venture out of doors and actually watch the horses, or dogs, go round at the track. Sydney's racetracks are very attractive, with good parking facilities, lots of grassed areas, plenty of bars, take-away food outlets, and restaurants, and the choice of investing your money on the Tote, or with a bookmaker. Children are welcome, and on a beautiful Sydney day it can be a great family day out.

The Horse-racing venues are:

Randwick Racecourse, Alison Road, Randwick,
ph 9663 8400.
Canterbury Racecourse, King Street, Canterbury,
ph 9799 8000.
Rosehill Racecourse, James Ruse Drive, Rosehill,
ph 9682 1000.

Warwick Farm Racecourse, Hume Highway, Warwick Farm, ph 9602 6199.

Races are held every Saturday and Wednesday at one of the above courses.
The first race is usually around 12.30, but during January and February the first race starts around 2.30pm. These are called *Twilight Meetings*, as the last race is around 6.30pm. The daily newspapers have details of race times, starters and jockeys, comprehensive form guides, TAB numbers and post positions.

Harness-racing venues are:

Harold Park Paceway, Ross Street, Glebe, ph 9660 3688. Meetings are held on Tuesday and Friday nights, and first race is 7pm.

Bankstown City Paceway, 178 Eldridge Road, Bankstown, ph 9708 4111. Meetings are held on Monday nights, and first race is 7pm.

Fairfield Paceway, Fairfield Showground, ph 9604 4559. Meetings are not held on a regular basis, so either phone the club or look in the newspapers for forthcoming races.

Greyhound racing is held at *Wentworth Park*, Wentworth Park Road, Glebe, ph 9660 6232. Meetings are held every Monday and Saturday nights and the first race is 7.30pm.

Shopping

The 'City'

Sydney has a large shopping area in the city, stretching from Park Street in the south to Hunter Street, with shops along George, Pitt, Castlereagh and Elizabeth Streets, which run south-north, and Market, King and Hunter Streets, which run roughly east-west. The section of Pitt Street between Market and King Streets is a pedestrian mall, with many arcades connecting it to both Castlereagh and George Streets. The closest railway stations to the shopping areas are Town Hall, Wynyard, St James and Martin Place.

If on the day you have set aside to shop, the heavens open and the rain pours down, remember *it is possible to walk from Town Hall Station to the MLC Centre in Martin Place without venturing out of doors.* It is rather a convoluted route, but there are signs pointing you in the right direction. Basically, from the station take the arcade under the Queen Victoria Building to Grace Bros, then from the first floor of GBs take the overpass to Centrepoint, then travel across the Imperial Arcade, Glasshouse and Skygarden shopping centres to the King Street overpass, and, voilá, you are in the MLC Centre. Of course, if the weather is warm and sunny, forget this option and stroll through the Mall.

Shops are normally open Mon-Wed 9am-5.30pm, Thurs 9am-9pm, Fri 9am-6pm, Sat 9am-5pm, Sun 11am-5pm, but this is not a hard and fast rule. Some open earlier and close later, particularly on Sunday, and many suburban supermarkets are open until late at night six days a week, and until around 6pm on Sunday. The shops in the tourist areas are open every day, usually with extended hours.

Souvenirs

If you are only interested in buying souvenirs, such as

cuddly koalas and kangaroos, T-shirts, etc, it is probably best to head for the tourist areas, such as **The Rocks** and **Darling Harbour**, or **Circular Quay**.

Other 'typically Sydney' souvenirs are found in the range of goods at the Done Art & Design Shops at The Rocks, Darling Harbour, Queen Victoria Building and the departure level of the International Airport. Ken Done is a local artist who produces very colourful works of art featuring the harbour, the bridge, the opera house, koalas, kangaroos, etc. These paintings are reproduced on material and his wife, Judy, designs a spectacular range of sportswear, swimwear, homewares, bags, stationery - in fact, just about everything you can think of can be found in their shops.

Buying Opals

If you have your heart set on some **opal jewellery,** you should grab your passport and airline ticket and head for a duty free store, or a jewellery shop that has a 'Tax Free for Overseas Visitors' sign in the window. In the case of opals, which are mined in Australia and set in jewellery locally, there is no duty, therefore in both establishments you would be saving the sales tax only (approx 30%).

Australia produces more than 90% of the world's opals, and the three main areas where they are found are Lightning Ridge in NSW which produces the Black Opal; Quilpie, where the Queensland Boulder Opal originates; and Coober Pedy in South Australia, which has the White or Milk Opal.

When buying opals there are a few important terms you should know:

Solid Opal - this is the most valuable, and is good for investment purposes. The more colourful and complete, the greater its value.

Doublet - this is comprised of slices of opal glued together, and is of medium value. It has no investment value.

Triplet - slices of opal covered with quartz, perspex or glass. This is the least expensive with no investment value.

If your pocket can't stretch as far as a solid opal, but you still would like a piece of opal jewellery, remember that anything that is glued can come unstuck, and that condensation can form under perspex or glass. The less expensive types of opal are not suitable for rings, unless you are going to remember to take them off every time you wash your hands.

Department Stores

David Jones

David Jones has two stores in the city - one bounded by Elizabeth, Market and Castlereagh Streets, the other diagonally opposite on the corner of Market and Castlereagh Streets. The Elizabeth Street store is devoted mainly to ladies' wear, except for the Lower Ground Floor (haberdashery, books, records, CDs, pharmacy, confectionery, wool, fabrics and restaurant); the 5th Floor (toys, children's wear and sporting goods) and the 6th Floor (manchester).

The Market Street store is known as the men's store, but it also has the Food Hall on the lower ground floor, and stocks travel goods, and small and large electrical appliances and furniture. Both stores have the same phone number - 9266 5544.

David Jones was considered to be one of the most beautiful stores in the world, and was designed by the same person who later designed the refurbishment of Harrods in London, and there are similarities.

David Jones stores are open Mon-Fri 9am-5.30pm (Thurs to 9pm), Sat 9am-4pm, Sun 11am-5pm, and all major credit cards are accepted.

Grace Bros

Situated on the corner of George and Market Streets, Grace Bros is more of a family store and sells literally everything under one roof. It is now receiving a complete refit so it will be interesting to see its layout and the interior design upon completion. It has seven floors of shopping and is open Mon-Wed 8.30am-5.30pm, Thurs 8.30am-9pm, Fri 8.30am-6.30pm, Sat 8.30am-5pm, Sun 11am-5pm, ph 9238 9111.

The Argyle
Sydney's newest department store is situated in The Rocks. For more information see The Rocks section in the *City Sights* chapter.

City Shopping Centres

Town Hall Arcade
Situated underground in the Town Hall Station, there are two arcades of specialty shops. The shorter of the two from the station leads to Bathurst Street, near Kent Street, and the other continues under the Queen Victoria Building to Grace Bros.

The Queen Victoria Building
The QVB was built in 1898 in the Byzantine style, and originally housed the city markets. Bounded by George, Market, York and Druitt Streets, its prosperity was short-lived, and it fell into disrepair. At one stage it was used as part offices and part Municipal Library, and the partitions that succeeded in making the building into a rabbit warren were actually nailed onto the beautiful tiled floors. Both the inside and outside of the building were decidedly tacky, and in 1959 there was much debate about demolishing the entire structure and building another shrine to modern architecture. Fortunately, common sense prevailed and the wreckers were not allowed to move in, but it was not until 1982 that a 99-year lease was granted and over $75 million invested to restore the building to its original state.

It is a magnificent building, and Pierre Cardin, on a visit to Sydney, christened it "the most beautiful shopping centre in the world". But, it is not only a shopping centre, there are a lot of things to see, all with a royal theme, in keeping with the name of the building. It even has replicas of the Crown Jewels on the top level.

The Royal Automata Clock 'performs' on the hour between 9am and 9pm daily, and you need to get there early to see the moving Royal Pageant. (It is a good idea to keep a firm grip on your handbag and wallet while waiting in this crowd.)

The QVB is open seven days a week. Apart from the

range of boutiques and specialty shops, there are several restaurants and cafes, both in the QVB and in the underground walkway to Grace Bros.

Centrepoint
Advertised as being "the heart of the city", Centrepoint is located on Pitt Street Mall, beneath Sydney Tower, and connects Grace Bros with David Jones. It has 170 shops on four levels, including hairdressers, beauticians, leather shops, jewellery and accessory outlets, boutiques, and several coffee shops and takeaways. The lifts for the Sydney Tower are found on the elegant Gallery Level of Centrepoint.

The lower ground floor is the Centrepoint Tavern, a good spot for a quick lunch, or a happy-hour drink.

Centrepoint is open daily, but not all the shops are open outside normal shopping hours.

Imperial Arcade
The Imperial runs between the Pitt Street Mall and Castlereagh Street, and has 114 specialty shops on 3 levels. It is also connected to Centrepoint.

Glasshouse on The Mall
Located in the middle of the Pitt Street Mall, the Glasshouse has three floors of shopping, with the usual collection of boutiques, etc.

Skygarden
A very up-market shopping experience, Skygarden has three levels of prestigious shops under a huge crystal dome. The mosaic entrance arch is made of thousands of Venetian glass tiles, and depicts the day and night theme of the complex. The top dining level is nothing to write home about.

Strand Arcade
The Strand opened in 1892 and is an olde worlde walk-through with mosaic tiled floor and Victorian architecture. It connects Pitt Street Mall with George Street and is open Mon-Fri 9am-5.30pm, Sat 9am-4pm.

Mid City Centre

This centre connects Pitt Street Mall and George Street, and is between the Strand Arcade and Grace Bros, with an entrance from Grace Bros. It has four levels of shopping with over 40 fashion boutiques, more than 50 specialty shops, and first class restaurants and coffee shops.

MLC Centre

The MLC Centre has entrances from Martin Place, Castlereagh Street and King Street, and has fashion boutiques, coffee shops and restaurants, and the Theatre Royal. The outdoor cafes overlooking Martin Place are popular lunchtime places.

Royal Arcade

Located under the Sydney Hilton Hotel, the Royal Arcade is between Market and Park Streets, and connects Pitt and George Streets. It has a range of rather expensive shops, typical of those found in hotel arcades.

Piccadilly Arcade

The Piccadilly is near the Pitt Street Cinema Centre, and connects Pitt and Castlereagh Streets. It also has overhead walkway connections to the Sydney Hilton and Sheraton on the Park Hotels. This is another rather upmarket shopping experience.

At the other end of the shopping district, near Wynyard Station, there are a few more places waiting to be discovered.

Wynyard Arcade

Newly renovated, this arcade is situated inside the station and has specialty shops of its own as well as access to **Westpac Plaza** and the **Hunter Connection**.

Chifley Square

Situated on Hunter, Elizabeth and Phillip Streets, Chifley Square is home to, among other not-so-well-known names, the local branch of *Tiffany's*.

If after visiting all of the above you are still in a shopping mood, return to the city centre and hop on the monorail for: **Darling Harbour**.

Harbourside, Darling Harbour
Harbourside Festival Marketplace has 200 shops from boutiques to souvenirs, sportswear to art, and restaurants, cafes and bars. It is a bazaar for overseas visitors rather than for Sydneysiders.

Suburban Shopping Centres

Most suburbs have a shopping centre of some kind, although many consist of a supermarket, butcher, greengrocer and a few specialty shops, such as a haberdasher, a hardware outlet, delicatessen, etc.

Then there are suburbs that have giant shopping complexes with branches of one or both major department stores and many specialty shops.

Following is a list of these:

Bankstown Square Shopping Centre, North Terrace, Bankstown, ph 9790 0751.

Blacktown Westpoint Marketown, Patrick Street, Blacktown, ph 9621 3333.

Bondi Junction Westfield Shoppingtown, 500 Oxford Street, Bondi Junction, ph 9387 3333.

Burwood Westfield Shoppingtown, Burwood Road, Burwood, ph 9744 9596.

Carlingford Court Shopping Centre, cnr Pennant Hills & Carlingford Roads, ph 9871 4111.

Castle Tower, cnr Old Castle Hill Road & Eric Felton Street, Castle Hill, ph 9634 4911.

Chatswood Chase, 91 Archer Street, Chatswood, ph 9419 6255.

Chatswood Westfield Shoppingtown, cnr Anderson Street & Victoria Avenue, Chatswood, ph 9412 1555.

Hornsby Northgate Shopping Centre, cnr Florence & Hunter Streets, Hornsby, ph 9477 5111.

Hurstville Westfield Shoppingtown, cnr Cross Street & Park Road, Hurstville, ph 9570 6333.

Liverpool Westfield Shoppingtown, Macquarie Street, Liverpool, ph 9602 6633.

Macquarie Shopping Centre, cnr Herring & Waterloo Roads, North Ryde, ph 9887 3011.

Miranda Westfield Shoppingtown, 600 The Kingsway, Miranda, ph 9525 6344.

Pagewood Westfield Shoppingtown, cnr Wentworth Avenue & Bunnerong Road, ph 9344 6766.

Parramatta Westfield Shoppingtown, 159 Church Street, ph 9891 3929. This is the largest shopping centre in the Southern Hemisphere.

Roselands Shopping Centre, Roselands Drive, Roselands, ph 9750 0533.

Warringah Mall, Pittwater Road, Brookvale, ph 9905 0633.

Markets

The Rocks Market

Every Saturday and Sunday, at the end of George Street in The Rocks, a sail-like canopy transforms the area into a Portobello Road. It is not an exceptionally large market, but it has many interesting articles for sale, and the Victorian terraces, pubs and old warehouses that surround it contribute to a holiday atmosphere year round. Nearby there are plenty of cafes, outdoor food stalls and restaurants.

Paddy's Markets

There are two locations:

The original Paddy's is in Haymarket, near Chinatown. It is open Sat and Sun 9am-4pm.

The other is on Parramatta Road, Flemington, and it is open Fri 10am-4.30pm, Sun 9am-4.30pm.

There are over 1000 stalls in each location selling fashion garments, footwear, jewellery, household and electrical goods, takeaway foods, fresh fruit and vegetables, poultry, seafood, and heaps and heaps of souvenirs. Paddy's is the biggest market in Australia, and for further information, phone the Hotline - 11 589.

Parklea Markets

These markets are at the corner of Sunnyholt and Old Windsor Roads in Parklea, an outer suburb of Sydney. It is a big market with a wide variety of merchandise, and is worth a visit if you happen to be in the neighbourhood.

Paddington Bazaar

Located at the corner of Oxford and Newcombe Streets, Paddington, in the grounds of the Uniting Church, this bazaar is held on Saturdays 10am-4pm, ph 9331 2646. There are over 250 stalls offering all types of clothing, crafts, jewellery and food.

While you are in Paddington you could visit *Coo-ee Aboriginal Art*, 98 Oxford Street, ph 9332 1544. They have a large display of Aboriginal Art, and are agents for Tiwi Design fabrics.

Balmain Saturday Market

Held in the grounds of St Andrew's Congregational Church, corner Darling Street and Curtis Road, Balmain, every Saturday 7.30am-4pm, ph 9818 2674.

Glebe Markets

These are held in Glebe Public School, cnr Glebe Point Road & Derby Place, on Saturday 9am-4pm. Many think this Market has a lot of 'atmosphere'.

Common sight off Sydney's beaches.

Sport and Recreation

Boating

It should be noted that a licence is required to drive any mechanically driven vessel capable of 10 knots or more. There are several places around the harbour foreshores where bare boats can be hired. Here are a few names and addresses:

Abbotsford Point Boat Hire, 617 Great North Road, Abbotsford, ph 9713 8621.

Australian Sailing School & Club, Parrawi Road, Mosman, ph 9960 3077.

Balmoral Marine, 2 The Esplanade, Balmoral,
    ph 9969 6006.

Eastsail, d'Albora Marinas, New Beach Road, Rushcutters Bay, ph 9327 1166.

It's A Breeze Yacht Charter, The Spit, Mosman, ph 9960 3999.

Rose Bay Marina, 594 New South Head Road, Rose Bay, ph 9363 5930.

Cycling

Centennial Park On Wheels, 26 Clovelly Road, Randwick, ph 9314 6460, are open seven days and are close to Centennial Park. They hire out bikes at reasonable prices.

Golf

The closest golf course to the city is in **Moore Park,** on the corner of Cleveland Street and Anzac Parade, ph 9663 1064. It is an 18-hole course, par 71, 5790m.

Green fees: $18 Mon-Fri; $21 Sat-Sun.
Club hire: $25.
Buggy hire: $30 drive buggies; $4 pull buggies.

The club also has Twilight Rates, which begin at 2.30pm in winter and later in summer when daylight saving is in operation. They are:

Green fees: $12 Mon-Fri; $13 Sat-Sun.

Club hire: $15.
Buggy hire: $15 drive buggies; $2 pull buggies.
Other golf courses can be found listed in the Yellow
Pages of the Telephone Directory.

Horse Riding

Centennial Park Horse Hire, RAS Showground, Driver
Avenue, Moore Park, ph 9361 4513, has horses for hire
daily 9am-5pm. Centennial Park and adjoining Queens
Park have a combined area 220ha (543 acres) - more than
enough room to have a decent ride.

Ice Skating

The closest ice rink to the city is *Macquarie Ice Rink Pty Ltd*
in the Macquarie Shopping Centre, North Ryde,
ph 9888 1100.

Lawn Bowls

There are bowling clubs in almost every suburb of
Sydney, and one in the city. Bowling clubs are famous for
their hospitality, and visitors are warmly welcomed. It is
necessary, of course, to phone ahead to find out what
days are reserved for social play, and to organise for a set
of bowls. Bowling clubs are listed in the Yellow Pages of
the Telephone Directory under *Clubs - Bowling*. If you are
not sure which club is the closest to where you are
staying, you could contact the Royal NSW Bowling
Association, ph 9283 4555.

Roller Skating

The closest roller skating rink to the city is *Majestic
Rollarink*, 49 New Canterbury Road, Petersham, ph 9569
3233. It is open Tues-Fri 8-11pm, Sat-Sun noon-3pm.

Scuba Diving

Gear can be hired and dives arranged from the following:
Dive 2000, 2 Military Road, Neutral Bay, ph 9953 7783.
Deep 6 Diving Pty Ltd, 1057 Victoria Road, West Ryde,
ph 9858 4299.

Pro Dive, Head Office, 34/330 Wattle Street, Ultimo, ph 9281 6166.

Swimming

The closest public swimming pools to the city centre are:

North Sydney Olympic Pool, Alfred South Street, Milsons Point, ph 9955 2309;

Andrew (Boy) Charlton Pool, The Domain, Woolloomooloo, ph 9358 6686;

Prince Alfred Park Swimming Pool, Chalmers Street, Surry Hills (near Central Railway Station), ph 9319 7045.

The larger hotels have swimming pools, usually heated year round.

Tennis

Tennis courts abound in Sydney's suburbs and most have lights for night play. Pages of available courts can be found in the L-Z Yellow Pages of the Telephone Directory, appropriately enough under Tennis Courts For Hire. For spectators, the NSW Tennis Open is played at White City in Rushcutters Bay.

Ten Pin Bowling

The bowling centres close to the city are:

Balgowlah Bowling Centre, Condamine Street, Balgowlah, ph 9948 7656. Other centres can be found in the A-K Yellow Pages of the Telephone Directory under Ten Pin Bowling.

Spectator Sports

Basketball (April-October)

Sydney's team in the National Basketball League (NBL) is *The Kings*, and they play their home games at the Sydney Entertainment Centre. Contact the recorded Show Information line on 11 582, or enquiries, 9746 2969 for dates of the Kings' games.

Baseball (October-February)

The Sydney Blues is the local team in the National Baseball

League and their home games are played at the Parramatta Stadium. The teams in the local competition play at various suburban venues, and for information on games, times, etc, contact the NSW Baseball League on 9552 4635.

Cricket (October-March)

The Cricket Ground, near the Showground, is home to International matches, and is NSW's home ground in the Sheffield Shield competition played between the states. Grade matches are played on suburban grounds.

Football (March-October)

Rugby League is played on Saturdays and Sundays at various suburban grounds and at the Sydney Football Stadium, near the Showground.

Rugby Union is played on Saturdays at suburban grounds and at their headquarters at Concord Oval.

Soccer is played on Saturdays at various suburban grounds and Sydney Athletic Field, Anzac Parade, Kensington, ph 9662 4390.

Australian Football is played on Saturdays at suburban grounds, and the Sydney Swans play their home games in the Victorian competition at the Sydney Cricket Ground.

Horse Racing

See Entertainment.

Sydney Olympic Park

Although situated in the *demographic* heart of the city of Sydney, the Olympic Park is actually 14km from the CBD, in the suburb of Homebush.

Existing facilities include Bicentennial Park, the Sydney International Athletic and Aquatic Centres, a golf driving range, and the States Sport Centre. By mid-1999 the Olympic Stadium will be completed, as well as Tennis, Baseball and Archery Centres, and a Velodrome. A major metropolitan park, to be called Millennium Park, and an Olympic Village with accommodation for 15,000 athletes will be completed well before the 2000 deadline.

State Sports Centre

The Centre is a multi-purpose venue designed to present a full spectrum of events. The design enables the Centre to be used as: a competition venue for sporting events of State, National and International standard, and a training centre for these athletes; a sports education centre; and a venue for concerts, seminars, exhibitions, etc.

 The Arena, within the *Sports Hall*, is the focal point of the State Sports Centre, and is capable of staging a wide range of sports from gymnastics to showjumping, fencing to indoor cricket. It has seating for 5000, and a clear floor area of 57m x 38m.

 Also in the Sports Hall is the *Hall of Champions* which honours Australia's champs in many sports.

The State Softball Centre has two floodlit fields, warm-up facilities and accommodation for 3000 spectators.

 The State Hockey Centre has two synthetic pitches, flood lighting, and accommodation for 8000 spectators.

There are also outdoor netball courts, training centres and plans for many more sporting facilities. When Sydney hosts the 2000 Olympic Games, the Centre on Homebush Bay will become world famous.

For information about current programs at the Centre, phone their 24-hour Information line, 9746 2855.

At present transport to the Olympic Site is by car, bus or river cat, but plans include a rail service with a three platform station in close proximity to the major sporting facilities. The rail service is expected to be operating in time for the 1998 Royal Easter Show.

 Guided tours of the Olympic Site are available Mon-Fri at 9.30am, 10.30am and 12.30pm. Tours on the Homebush Bay Shuttle bus service start at the north side of Strathfield Station and take about 45 minutes. For more information, ph 9735 4800.

Beaches

Sydney's coastline stretches for approximately 65km, from Palm Beach in the north, to Cronulla in the south. Most Sydneysiders have their 'favourite' beach, which is not necessarily the closest to their homes. Some people grew up living near one beach, then moved as an adult to another, but you will usually find them returning to their original haunt.

Most of the ocean beaches are patrolled during the summer months on the weekends and during school holidays. The lifesavers, who know what they are doing, erect flags in the safest part of the beaches, and people are requested to make sure they swim between these flags. If they don't, and get into difficulties, the lifesavers are not going to let them drown, but it would serve them right if they did.

If the beach is considered unsafe, eg because of a strong undertow, or a very high tide, the lifesavers will close it, and erect a sign warning people not to enter the water. Take notice of this sign and decide to spend the day somewhere else.

Board riders are given their own stretch of beach, so that they don't interfere with swimmers, and swimmers should keep out of the board area.

Lifesavers in this country are not paid for the hours they spend on duty, they are young people who give freely of their time to keep our beaches safe.

Harbour beaches are not patrolled. It must not be assumed that the harbour is one giant swimming pool. There are several places where shark-nets have been strung across inlets, and these are the only places where you should venture into the water. You won't see one, but there are sharks in Sydney Harbour. It is generally believed that old sharks that can't fend for themselves in the open sea, come into the harbour for easy feeding, and what could be easier than a human thrashing around. Of course, there are also sharks in the ocean, but the surf patrols on these beaches keep a sharp lookout, and sound alarms if a shark is sighted. You may not have caught a wave all day, but if a shark alarm sounds it is incredible how quickly you can get yourself back on the beach.

Having said all that, there has not been a shark attack in Sydney since 1963, when two children were taken whilst swimming in Middle Harbour.

Ocean Beaches

Listed below are the beaches stretching from Palm Beach in the north to Bundeena in the south, with the closest main road, and the public transport that gives access.

Also included is the following information for each venue:

Dressing Shed -	usually will include showers and toilets.
Patrolled -	in summer on weekends and during school holidays, ie from the first weekend in October to Easter the following year.
Pool -	rock pool suitable for children.
Board -	surf is suitable for board riders.
Surfers -	surf is suitable for body surfers.

Usually beaches back onto a park or a reserve, and there are clear directions on the major roads indicating the way to the beach. Most beaches tend to have some topless sunbathers during the hottest parts of the day!!

North of the Harbour

Palm Beach, off Barrenjoey Road, was once mainly frequented by the wealthy and yuppy set. It has now become very popular with British tourists because it is the setting for the TV series *Home and Away*. Dressing shed, patrolled, surfers and board, pool south end. About 1½ hours drive from the city centre.
Bus no 190 from Wynyard.

Whale Beach, off Barrenjoey Road. Dressing shed,

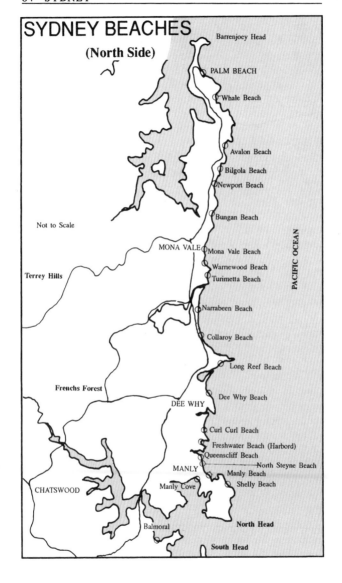

SYDNEY BEACHES
(North Side)

Barrenjoey Head

PALM BEACH

Whale Beach

Avalon Beach

Bilgola Beach

Newport Beach

Bungan Beach

Not to Scale

MONA VALE — Mona Vale Beach

Warnewood Beach

Turimetta Beach

Terrey Hills

PACIFIC OCEAN

Narrabeen Beach

Collaroy Beach

Long Reef Beach

Frenchs Forest

Dee Why Beach

DEE WHY

Curl Curl Beach

Freshwater Beach (Harbord)

Queenscliff Beach

North Steyne Beach

MANLY

Manly Beach

Manly Cove

Shelly Beach

CHATSWOOD

North Head

Balmoral

South Head

patrolled, surfers and board, pool south end. Bus 190 from Wynyard, Bus 193 from Avalon (infrequent service).

Avalon Beach, off Barrenjoey Road. Dressing shed, patrolled, surfers and board, pool south end.
Bus 190 from Wynyard.

Bilgola Beach, off Barrenjoey Road. Dressing shed, patrolled, surfers and board. Bus 190 from Wynyard.

Newport Beach, off Barrenjoey Road. Dressing shed, patrolled, surfers and board. Bus 190 from Wynyard.

Bungan Beach, off Barrenjoey Road. Patrolled, board. Bus 190 from Wynyard.

Mona Vale Beach, off Barrenjoey Road. Top end not patrolled (Bongin Bongin). Dressing shed, patrolled south end, surfers south end, board north end. Bus 157 from Manly, Bus 184 from Wynyard (peak hour).

Warriewood Beach, off Pittwater Road. Dressing shed, patrolled surfers and board. Bus 157 from Manly.

Turimetta Beach, off Pittwater Road. Not patrolled, board. Bus 155 and 157 from Manly.

Narrabeen Beach, off Pittwater Road. Dressing shed, patrolled, surfers and board. Buses 182 and 190 from Wynyard, Bus 155 and 157 from Manly.

Collaroy Beach, off Pittwater Road adjoining Narrabeen Beach. Dressing shed, patrolled, surfers and board, pool southern end. Bus 182 and 190 from Wynyard. Bus 155 and 157 from Manly.

Collaroy Basin, off Pittwater Road. Surfers, little swell.

Long Reef Beach, off Pittwater Road. Dressing shed, patrolled, surfers and board. Bus 182 and 190 from Wynyard, Bus 155 and 157 from Manly.

Dee Why Beach, Howard Street, off Pittwater Road, adjoins Long Reef Beach. Dressing shed, patrolled, surfers and board, pool south end. Bus 178 and 180 from Queen Victoria Building, Bus 190, 182, 184 from Wynyard.

Curl Curl Beach, Oliver Road, off Pittwater Road. Dressing shed, patrolled, surfers and board, pool south end. Bus 136 from Manly.

Freshwater (Harbord) Beach, Oliver Road, via Pittwater Road. dressing shed, patrolled, surfers and board, pool north end. Bus 139 from Manly.

Queenscliff Beach, off Pittwater Road. Dressing shed, patrolled, surfers and board, pool north end. Bus 136 and 139 from Manly.

North Steyne Beach, off Pittwater Road, adjoins Queenscliff Beach. Dressing shed, patrolled, surfers and board. See Manly Beach for travel information.

Manly Beach, off Pittwater Road, adjoins North Steyne Beach. Dressing shed, patrolled, surfers and board. Bus 143 and 144 from Chatswood, Ferry from Circular Quay, JetCat from Circular Quay. Peak hour bus services available from Wynyard.

Shelly Beach, off Darley Road. Sheltered area with little swell, suitable for swimmers. Between Shelly Beach and Manly Beach there is a pool at Fairy Bower.

South of the Harbour

Bondi Beach, via Bondi Road off Old South Head Road. Dressing shed, patrolled, surfers and board, sanctioned topless area south end, pool at south end. Bus 380 and 389 from Circular Quay, 365 from Edgecliff.

An internationally famous beach, Bondi attracts more than 40,000 people on any given sunny Sunday afternoon. The 1km strip of beach has a long history of development since the local government authority gained control of it in 1881. By 1907 it was very popular with the neck-to-knee fraternity, although bathing time was limited to half an hour to avoid loitering. In 1928, the Bondi Beach Pavilion was built and then contained changing rooms for 1200 people, turkish baths, shops, a gymnasium and a ballroom. Today it is a community centre.

Surf life saving had its origins here and at nearby Bronte, with these clubs claiming to be the world's oldest. Surf Carnivals are often held at the beach, but the standard of the surf depends on the wind, and can range from enormous waves on day to a mill-pond the next.

Tamarama Beach. Off Bronte Road. Dressing shed, surfers and board. Bus 360 and 361 from Bondi Junction.

Bronte Beach, off Bronte Road. Squeezed between tamarama and Clovelly it can some rough surf at times. Dressing shed, patrolled, surfers and board, pool south end. Bus 378 from Railway Square.

Clovelly Beach, off Clovelly Road. Dressing shed, patrolled. Bus 339 and 340 from Millers Point. Although Clovelly has a sandy foreshore, it is more like a swimming pool than a beach. Good for children.

Coogee Beach, off Coogee Bay Road. Dressing shed, patrolled, surfers and board, pool south end. Bus 372 from Railway Square, Bus 373 from Circular Quay (Pitt Street).

Maroubra Beach, Fitzgerald Avenue, off Anzac Parade. Dressing shed, patrolled, surfers and board. Bus 395 from Railway Square, Bus 396 from Circular Quay.

Wanda Beach, off The Kingsway. Dressing shed, patrolled, surfers and board. You catch a train to Cronulla and then make the short walk to beach.

Elouera Beach, adjoins Wanda Beach. Dressing shed, patrolled, surfers and board, pool south end. Train to Cronulla, walk to beach.

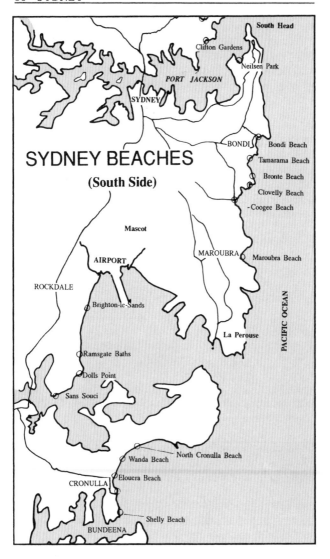

SYDNEY BEACHES
(South Side)

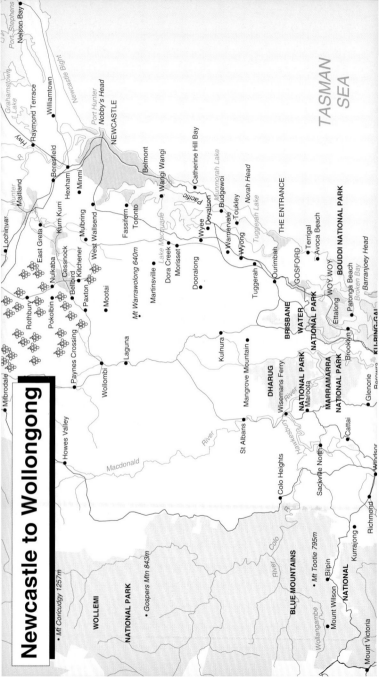

Newcastle to Wollongong

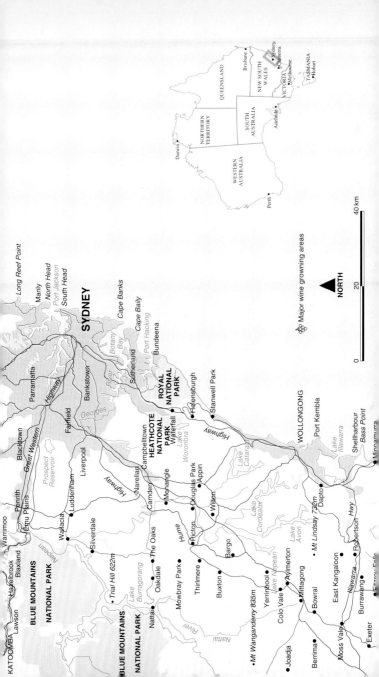

North Cronulla Beach, adjoins Wanda and Elouera Beaches, off The Kingsway. Dressing shed, patrolled, surfers and board, pool south end. Train to Cronulla, walk to beach.

South Cronulla Beach, off The Kingsway. Dressing shed, patrolled, surfers and board, pool north end. Train to Cronulla, walk to beach.

Shelly Beach, off Cronulla Street. Dressing shed, patrolled, surfers and board, pool south end. Train to Cronulla, walk to beach.

Harbour Beaches

There are hundreds of coves and bays around the harbour, but we are only including those that have shark-proof nets, changing facilities, takeaway food outlets, and picnic areas. Obviously the beaches on the harbour do not have waves.

Clifton Gardens, Chowder Bay. The bay is two bays north-east of Taronga Park Zoo, and not easy to get to by public transport. Bus 228 from Milsons Point (Mon-Fri), Bus 247 from Wynyard/QVB to Taronga Zoo, alight at Thompson Street and follow the signs.

Balmoral, Hunter's Bay. This is quite a pretty beach and is divided into two by Rocky Point, a tree-covered outcrop. Balmoral is very popular and has takeaway food bars as well as coffee shops and an up-market restaurant. The rotunda on the beach is used for many shows on summer evenings, the 'Shakespeare on the Beach' programs in particular have a large following.
    Bus 238 from Taronga Zoo, Bus 257 from Chatswood, or Bus 233 from Mosman Wharf.

Manly Cove, Manly. The swimming enclosure is adjacent to Manly Wharf, where the ferry from Circular Quay docks. Travel by ferry, or Bus 144 from Chatswood.

(Facing) Sydney Harbour Bridge at sunset [above], Sydney Opera House lit for the Olympic quest; Facing p.88 Manly Beach

Nielsen Park, between Vaucluse Road and Greycliffe Avenue, Vaucluse, in the eastern suburbs. During the swimming season (October to April) a shark-proof net is erected at Shark Beach. Experience has shown that this net must be taken down during the colder months because it cannot withstand the winter storms and heavy seas. There are dressing sheds and showers for swimmers, and a kiosk is situated opposite the beach. Ferry from Circular Quay, Bus 325 from Circular Quay.

Botany Bay Beaches

Botany Bay was where Captain James Cook landed, and where Captain Phillip was sent to begin the new colony. Phillip, unable to find a fresh water supply, sailed further north to Sydney Harbour. Nowadays Botany Bay is a densely populated area, and if you arrived in Sydney by air, you have already spotted it. Kingsford Smith Airport is situated on the shores of Botany Bay.

The Bay also has its share of sharks, so if you feel like a swim, stick to one of the following.

Brighton-le-Sands Baths, off Grand Parade. It has wire netting for protection, although the rest of the Lady Robinson Beach is not protected and is frequented by swimmers. There are dressing sheds. Bus 302-303 from Circular Quay, Bus 478 from Rockdale.

Bundeena

South of Botany Bay is Port Hacking. Cronulla is on its northern side, and Bundeena on the southern side borders the Royal National Park. Access is by ferry from Cronulla. Surrounding Bundeena are Hordens, Gunyah and Jobbons, pleasant but small beaches which have little swell and are suitable only for swimming. They have no safety nets and are not patrolled.

City Sights

It is not possible to see the sights of the city of Sydney in one day on a walking tour, even if you are super-fit. Apart from the distance, Sydney is not a flat city, and the hills would slow you down. By taking advantage of **The Sydney Explorer** bus you could catch a glimpse of everything, but you still wouldn't have time to appreciate what you saw. It is best to allot at least a few days for the city itself before you spread your wings to the outer attractions. So this guide is set out in areas, perhaps you should allow one day per area.

Note that all museums are closed on Christmas Day and Good Friday.

Circular Quay Area

Sydney Harbour Bridge

Affectionately known to Sydneysiders as 'The Coathanger' the Sydney Harbour Bridge dominates the city skyline. It is 503m long, and was completed in 1932 after nine years in the making. It was built from either shore, and when the two halves met they were only 7.6cm (3 inches in the old measurements) out of alignment! The Bridge opened with a piece of drama. The dignitaries were lined up, the Premier, Jack Lang, stepped forward to cut the ribbon, and up rode Captain de Groot on a noble steed. He slashed the ribbon with his sword, and all and sundry stood speechless, at least for a few seconds. The miscreant was apprehended, the ribbon was rejoined, and the ceremony continued.

In August, 1992, came the opening of the long-awaited harbour tunnel, which has lived up to its expectations in reducing peak hour traffic snarls on the bridge. You can't walk through the tunnel but you can walk over the bridge, and you can climb up the south-east pylon for some of the best harbour views. The pylon is open daily 10am-5pm and admission is $2 adult, 50c children.

From the bridge there is a good view of Sydney's

Glebe Island Bridge

newest crossing, the **Glebe Island Bridge**, which has improved the traffic flow into the city from the west.

Sydney Opera House

The magnificent performing arts complex is situated on Bennelong Point, which was named by Governor Phillip after an Aboriginal he befriended, taught English, and actually took back to England. This spot is apparently where Bennelong had his humpy.

Shrouded in controversy during its construction, Sydney Opera House was finally completed in 1973, and has since become almost the symbol of Australia. Instantly recognisable anywhere because of its unique architecture, it can only really be appreciated when seen as part of its surroundings. Then it seems to become another form of sea-going craft, and it doesn't take too much imagination to picture it joining the other sail boats on the harbour.

The Opera House has four theatres, four restaurants and six bars, and is surrounded by wide walkways. Details of current programs are published in the daily newspapers, and the Box Office is open Mon-Sat 9am-8.30pm and two hours prior to the start of a Sunday performance. Phone bookings may be made up to seven days prior to the performance, and the booking clerk will advise when payment must be made, or you can use your credit card. Guided tours are available daily 9am-4pm. They last one hour and cost $9 adult, $6 concession. Concessions are available to children, Australian Pensioners and students of all nationalities.

There are also tours on some Sundays only that take visitors backstage. The availability of the backstage tours depends on whether there are rehearsals in the house. It is advisable to contact Guided Tours (ph 9250 7250) on the Saturday before you would like to tour. The cost of these is $13.50 per person, there are no concessions, and the tours are unsuitable for children under 12.

Bus no 438 travels down George Street to the concourse. Circular Quay Railway Station is the closest stop for train passengers.

Circular Quay

It doesn't seem to matter when you visit the Quay, there are always lots of people around, but it is on weekends and holidays that you have the added colour and noise of all the buskers. From men playing classical pieces on violins, to little kids belting it out on a range of brass instruments, to aborigines and (non aborigines) playing didgeridoos and teaching people to perform kangaroo and emu dances - it's all great entertainment.

It is a real 'mezcla' of people waiting for ferries to take them to Manly or the Zoo for the day; people hurrying to catch their train at the railway station; some buying tickets for harbour cruises; some fishing in the doubtful water near Wharf 5; others, the well-dressed ones, are beginning their walk around to the Opera House for a ballet or opera matinee.

Circular Quay Railway Station, although not underground, is part of the City Circle, and the Cahill Expressway on top of the railway takes traffic from the Bridge to the Eastern Suburbs and Macquarie Street.

Justice & Police Museum

This museum, at 8 Phillip Street, ph 9252 1144, is almost directly opposite Wharf 5, and if you look across you will see figures of 'burglars' seemingly trying to break into the building on the corner. It is only open Sunday 10am-5pm, but is worth a visit if you are in the area. The collection began with the Police Exhibition that was an exhibit at the Royal Easter Show for many years. It is now housed in a former police station and court house, and has displays of relics from police investigations and trials, as well as record sheets of some of Sydney's most notorious felons. Admission is $5 adults, $3 children.

Museum of Sydney

Situated on the corner of Phillip and Bridge Streets, on the site of First Government House, this modern museum is open daily 10am-5pm and admission is $6 adults, $4 children, $15 family, ph 9251 5988. It has an excellent cafe and a good bookshop, both of which can visited without entering the museum. The bookshop specialises in architecture and design titles. There are also exhibits in the forecourt, and in the entrance foyer the foundations of Australia's first Government House are visible. There has been some controversy about the exhibits on show, and about the quotations of famous people that are on display throughout the galleries.

Museum of Contemporary Art

The MCA is the Art Deco building on the waterfront around from Wharf 5. It formerly housed the Maritime Services Board and when the board moved to new premises, there was some talk of levelling this imposing structure. Then it was realised that it would be the perfect place for the J.W. Power collection of contemporary art, which had been left to the University of Sydney many years before. Now the museum is run as a non-profit company jointly by the University and the NSW Government. The museum's brochure says, "This is a museum about the beautiful under our noses, the unusual, the weird and wacky in the visual, electronic, sound and tactile world we all live in." And that just about sums it up! The museum is open daily 10am-6pm, and admission is $8 adult, $5 child under 16, $18 family, ph 9241 5892 (recorded information). Entrance is from the Quay or from George Street.

The MCA Store in George Street has an incredible range of books, magazines, posters, etc, and the MCA Cafe next to the Quay entrance is worth a visit in itself, and why not? It is managed by the people from the award-winning restaurant, Rockpool, which is nearby at 109 George Street, The Rocks.

Cadman's Cottage

Continuing along the waterfront, the cottage is situated in a reserve on the corner of Argyle Street. It is the oldest remaining house in Sydney, and was home to John Cadman, the last Government Coxswain. The two-storey sandstone cottage was finished in early 1816, and building was possibly supervised by Francis Greenway, the convict architect, who lived nearby. At that time the house stood two metres from the water, on a small sandy beach, and had a wharf on its northern side. Its present position resulted in the late 1840s when ten acres of land were reclaimed to form Circular Quay. The lack of recorded history, artefacts or detailed plans of the cottage has stopped the National Parks & Wildlife Service (NPWS) from restoring the building as an historical museum. It is presently a NPWS shop, ph 9247 8861, and has plenty of brochures on walks and trips in Sydney parks and those further afield. It is open seven days a week.

The waterside walk continues around the back of the Overseas Terminal, where there are many tour offices, and from where bus tours depart, to Campbell's Cove, with many restaurants in converted storehouses; the wharf from which the *Bounty* and other cruise ships depart; and the Park Hyatt Sydney Hotel.

The Rocks Visitors Centre

Steps beside Cadman's Cottage lead up to George Street, and if you turn right at the top of the steps you will come to the old Sailors' Home which now houses The Rocks Visitor Centre, ph 9255 1788. The Centre is open daily 9am-5pm, and has a very good video presentation on the first floor, of the growth of Sydney from a small penal colony to a thriving modern city. They carry brochures and maps for tourist attractions all over Sydney.

George Street

Continuing along George Street, there are many old historic buildings and pubs, and on the weekends the Bridge end of the street is closed off and The Rocks Markets are held (see Shopping section).

In the building on the right hand side of the markets there are some interesting craft displays and shops.

Westpac Museum

Retrace your steps along George Street, walk past the Old Sydney Parkroyal Hotel, then turn up Playfair Street. Here at no 6-8 is the Westpac Museum, ph 9251 1419, which traces the history of the bank from its beginnings in 1817 as the Bank of NSW, to the present day of technological banking. There are also temporary exhibitions featuring subjects as diverse as the Royal Flying Doctor Service and Antarctica. The museum is open, Tues-Fri 10.30am-4pm, Sat-Mon 1-4pm and admission is free.

By the way, Playfair Street bends to the left, and straight ahead from the museum is Atherden Place, with four terrace houses. It is the shortest street in Sydney.

The Rocks Square

The square is in the middle of Playfair Street (which is closed to traffic) and this area has many outdoor eateries, jazz or rock bands, little shops, and several lanes leading here, there and everywhere. Following Playfair Street to its end brings you to Argyle Street.

The Rocks Puppet Cottage

The cottage is situated in Kendall Lane, and can be reached from George Street through a lane at no 77. It is open 10am-5pm Wed-Sun, ph 9241 2902. There are hundreds of puppets on display, and shows are held at 11am, 12.30pm, 2pm and 3.30pm on weekends, and other days during school holidays. Admission is free, and the cottage is sponsored by the Sydney Cove Authority.

Susannah Place
Situated at 58-64 Gloucester Street, Susannah Place is a terrace of four brick houses that was built in 1844. It is now a museum of the life-style in the area from the 1840s until the turn of the century. Included is a shop that stocks the type of goods that would have been available then.

The Rocks Centre
The centre is on the corner of Playfair & Argyle Streets and offers two floors of boutiques and eateries.

The Argyle
The Rocks' newest addition is The Argyle Department Store which has around 5000 square metres of upmarket shopping. Modelled along the lines of France's Galleries Lafeyette, the different departments are managed by individual operators, but blend to give the appearance of one entity.

The building was completed in 1828 using convict labour, and was the first Customs House in Australia. Over the years it has had several uses, and names, until in 1993 it was completely restored by the Sydney Cove Authority at a cost of around $9 million. In 1994 it was offered for lease as a department store, and in October 1996 the Argyle opened its doors to customers.

A few doors up Argyle Street is **The Argyle Tavern**, which is open daily 11.30am-3pm, 7.30-10.30pm, ph 9247 7782. This is a real Aussie theatre-restaurant, that serves good old fashioned tucker (food) with large helpings of fun and laughter.

Clocktower Square
The square is the building on the corner of Argyle and Harrington Streets with the clocktower, and it contains several souvenir shops, a Japanese restaurant, and **The Rocks Opal Mine**, ph 9247 4974. Here you can not only buy tax-free opals, you can dig for them! There is a mine shaft elevator which really does seem to travel down to the depths of the earth, then the door opens and an old mine tunnel appears with 'miners' busy at work. It's good

fun even if you are not interested in buying opals, and is open seven days.

The Rocks Walking Tours

The office, and the departure point for the tours, is at 106 George Street, ph 9247 6678. There are three tours Mon-Fri, at 10.30am, 12.30pm and 2.30pm, and two tours Sat-Sun at 11.30am and 2.30pm, and it is wise to ring beforehand to make sure there are vacancies. The tours last about an hour and a quarter, and could be classified as 'strolls', so don't be put off if your fitness level is not what is should be. Every aspect of the history of The Rocks is covered, and changes made over the years are highlighted. Costs are $10 adults, $6.50 children 10-16, children under 10 free.

Millers Point

Millers Point is the suburb on the other side of the Harbour Bridge, and Bradfield Highway which crosses it, to The Rocks. It can be reached by following Hickson Road from the Park Hyatt Sydney Hotel around the base of the south-east pylon of the Bridge to Dawes Point; by following George Street to its end, then walking down steps to Hickson Road; or by continuing along Argyle Street and passing under the Bradfield Highway.

The closest attraction to the Bridge is **Pier One**, a three-level structure which was full of shops when it was first opened, but is now visited more for its restaurants - *Harbour Watch*, *Water's Edge* and the *Harbourside Brasserie*, which is also a nightclub. Pier One does have a large amusement arcade, a book shop, and some galleries where artists can sometimes be seen at work.

The **Holy Trinity (Garrison) Church** is in Argyle Street. It was built in 1848 and is called the Garrison Church because it was compulsory for the soldiers of the 50th Regiment stationed at Dawes Point Battery to attend the morning service. There is a leaflet available for purchase ($2) at the rear of the church which details its complete history.

Argyle Place, the little park just up the street, is Sydney oldest village green.

Sydney Observatory is on Watson Road, Observatory Hill, and can be reached by following Argyle Street, then walking up some steep steps. The Observatory, ph 9217 0485, has a regular program of exhibitions, films, talks and night viewings, and a hands-on exhibition. During the day it is open Mon-Fri 2-5pm, Sat-Sun 10am-5pm and admission is free. It is also open nightly, except Wednesday, and has two programs in winter (6.15 and 8.15pm) and one in summer (8.15pm). Bookings are necessary for the night sessions, and charges are $6 adults, $3 children, $15 family.

You may wonder about the ball on top of the building. It has been part of the synchronisation of time in Sydney since the building was erected in 1858. In the early days of the colony, a gun was fired at exactly 1pm from Dawes Point, and another from Fort Denison. These were for the ships in the harbour to check their chronometers. To enable the settlers in the colony to also check their time-pieces, the ball on the Observatory was hoisted by mechanical means to the top of the pole at approximately five minutes to one, then when the guns fired, the ball dropped back to the bottom. The ball still fulfils its function, but only on special occasions such as public holidays and during school holidays.

The **S.H. Ervin Gallery** is in the National Trust Centre, almost next door to the Observatory. The building was erected in 1815 as a military hospital, then for many years was home to one of Sydney's leading girls' high schools.

The Gallery has changing exhibitions, and for current programs and entry charges phone 9258 0123 (weekends 9258 0173).

Taronga Park Zoo

The Zoo's address is Bradley's Head Road, ph 0055 20218 (time charged) or 9969 2777, but the most scenic way to get there is by ferry from Circular Quay. They leave from

> Entry to the zoo is $14.95 adult, $7.50 child, $36 family, and it is open every day 9am-5pm.
> A ZooPass is available and includes ferry, aerial/bus ride and entry. It costs $21 adult, $10.40 child.

Wharf 4 (but check the signs because this can change) every half hour, and the trip takes 12 minutes.

Taronga has Australia's best collection of native and exotic animals, and also offers some of the finest views of the city, particularly from near the giraffe enclosure. There are seal shows, a rainforest aviary, a nocturnal house, all the usual animals, and Friendship Farm, where children can pat baby animals.

Throughout the park there are plenty of food outlets, and there is also a licensed restaurant. The zoo is built on a hill, so it is best to take the bus or the aerial safari ride from the wharf to the top entrance, then view all the animals on the walk back down to the wharf.

The Botanical Gardens and Macquarie Street

The Botanical Gardens

The Gardens are a popular lunchtime spot for city workers, and weekends see many family picnics. They are situated on the edge of Farm Cove, where the early colonists first tried to grow vegetables.

As you enter through the gate near the Opera House and climb the slight slope, the castle to your right is **Government House**. Built between 1837 and 1845, this is the most sophisticated example of a Gothic Revival building in New South Wales. The House is now used by the Governor only for official receptions, dinners and investitures, and is open to the public Fri-Sun 10am-3pm, ph 9931 5222. The garden belonging to the House is open every day 10am-4pm.

The building at the end of the driveway leading from Government House is the **Conservatorium of Music**, which was originally the Governor's stables.

Signposts point the way to **Mrs Macquarie's Chair**, a rock outcrop where the Governor's wife apparently sat to

Entrance to Taronga Park Zoo

watch for ships arriving from England. The island fort you can see is **Fort Denison**, also known as Pinchgut, because the island was used for a short time as a place of punishment for erring convicts. The fort was built as part of Sydney's defences, and has recently come under the jurisdiction of the National Parks and Wildlife Service, as part of Sydney Harbour National Park. Tours of Fort Denison leave from Wharf 6, Circular Quay, but must be booked in advance, ph 9206 1166.

The footpath by the sea wall leads to the visitors centre and shop, a kiosk, and a restaurant; and signposts show the way to the herbarium, the pyramid glasshouse and other exhibits. There are two exits near the pyramid, one on to Macquarie Street, the other leads to the Art Gallery. The gardens are open daily 8am to sunset, ph 9231 8125.

Art Gallery of New South Wales
The Art Gallery is in Art Gallery Road, in the Botanic Gardens, and faces The Domain. It is a spectacular building, and houses a vast contemporary collection of

Australian, European and Asian Art, and a fine collection of Aboriginal paintings and artifacts. Many special exhibitions are held at the Gallery, and for recorded information on current exhibits phone 9225 1790. Free guided tours of the Gallery are available - check at the information desk on your left as you walk into the gallery through the vestibule. There is no charge for admission to the Gallery and its permanent collection, but a fee is levied for special exhibitions.

There is a restaurant and a coffee shop, and the Gallery is open daily, 10am-5pm.

The Domain
The Domain is the large grassed area between the Art Gallery and the Public Library. It is a peaceful park setting for soap box orators on Sundays, and the venue for a number of Sydney's free summertime open-air concerts, such as Opera In The Park.

State Library of New South Wales
The original, imposing building of the Library faces Shakespeare Place, on the corner of Macquarie Street, and the new section has been built behind, but can also be entranced from Macquarie Street.

The Library contains the nation's finest collection of Australian history, and an excellent Reference Library. The new wing contains the latest technology for reading and learning. The information desk has a self-guided tour sheet which has information on every part of the library, and is worth obtaining.

There is a restaurant and a bookshop, and the Library is open Mon-Fri 9am-9pm, Sat 9am-5pm, Sun 11am-5pm, and admission is free, ph 9230 1414. The Library has changing exhibitions, usually of an historic nature, and information on current programs can be obtained from a recorded information phone line, 0055 21068 (0055 calls are time-charged).

Parliament House
Situated in Macquarie Street, Parliament House is open to visitors, and they can even attend a session. Parliament

generally sits from mid-February to early May, and from mid-September to early December, on Tues, Wed and Thurs. For information on hours, ph 9230 2111.

The Mint
Sydney Hospital is between Parliament House and The Mint Museum, which was once a wing of Governor Macquarie's Rum Hospital. Built in 1816, it was the 1850s that earned the building its name for it was here that gold sovereigns were coined. Visitors can visit the Mint's former vaults, strike their own souvenir coin, and learn how raw gold was turned into bullion and currency. The Mint is open daily 10am-5pm and admission is $5 adult, $2 children, $12 family, ph 9217 0311.

Hyde Park Barracks
The Barracks is a Georgian building, designed by convict architect Francis Greenway, and was intended as convict accommodation when it was built in 1819. It now houses an impressive collection which shows how the convicts spent their daily lives, where and how they slept, ate and worked. The Barracks also has the Greenway Gallery, which has changing exhibitions of historical and cultural interest. The Barracks Cafe is in the original confinement cell area and has an imaginative menu, but it's a bit on the expensive side.

The Historic Houses Trust of New South Wales has control of the Barracks which is open daily (except Christmas Day and Good Friday) 10am-5pm, ph 9223 8922. Admission is $5 adults, $3 children, $12 family.

Francis Greenway also designed St James' Anglican Church on the other side of the street from the Barracks.

St Mary's Cathedral
The Cathedral is a magnificent example of revival Gothic architecture in Hawkesbury sandstone. Begun in 1866, after a fire destroyed the previous church, the workmen laid down their tools in 1928, after 62 years of work. The twin spires over the southern nave were never added, giving the exterior an unfinished look, but the interior is beautiful and fascinating, with its soaring vaults,

gargoyles, side altars and statues.

The outstanding feature is the stained glass windows which have scenes from the life of the Blessed Virgin Mary, and the early days of the Catholic Church in Australia. Under the Cathedral is a crypt where the Catholic Archbishops of Sydney are interred, and there is also an exhibition on the background of the Cathedral and the plans for its future.

The Chapter Hall is the earliest building on the site. Built in Gothic Revival style between 1843 and 1845, it was to form part of a Benedictine Monastery planned to include the original cathedral. The monastery was never completed. The Chapter Hall was commissioned by John Bede Polding, the first Archbishop of Sydney, and since its construction it has been used as a meeting hall, classics school and general purpose hall. It is classified by the National Trust.

Another attraction of the Cathedral is its world-famous choir which sings every Sunday at the 10.30am Mass.

Hyde Park

Opposite Hyde Park Barracks is Queen's Square with an imposing statue of Queen Victoria, and adjoining that is Hyde Park and the beautiful Archibald Fountain.

Hyde Park is bounded by Queen's Square, College Street, Liverpool Street and Elizabeth Street, with Park Street running through the centre, and changing its name to William Street as it crosses College Street.

At the Queen's Square end of the park there are entrances to the underground St James Station from Macquarie Street, Elizabeth Street (at the end of Market Street) and Queen's Square. At the Liverpool Street end of the park there are entrances to the underground Museum Station from Elizabeth Street (at the end of Bathurst Street) and near the corner of Elizabeth and Liverpool Streets. Near here is also the **Anzac War Memorial** with the tomb of the Unknown Soldier.

The Australian Museum

The Museum is at 6 College Street, and is open daily, except Christmas Day, 9.30am-5pm. General admission to the museum is $5 adult, $2 child (5-15), $12 family, but for special temporary exhibitions there may be an extra fee. There is no charge after 4pm each day. The Museum Alive Line, ph 0055 29408, gives all details of current attractions, special programs for children, etc, and gives information on guided tours and any query you could possibly have.

The Australian Museum is recognised as one of the foremost museums of its type in the world, and has a bookshop and restaurant.

Parking

It is not really recommended that you take your car to the city if you intend to visit several places. Wherever you find a place to park, you will be walking quite a distance away from it, then have to retrace your steps to retrieve it. There is very limited long term street parking, and although there are parking stations in The Rocks area (behind the Regent Hotel), it could end up costing you more for the car than for your day out.

Another alternative is the council-run **Domain Parking Station,** which is entered from Sir John Young Crescent, east of St Mary's Cathedral.

This station is open Mon-Sat 7am-9pm, Sun 10am-6pm, and charges are: Mon-Fri, 1st three hours $4 per hour, 4th hour $2 (maximum of $14); Sat-Sun $6 per day.

There is a moving underground footway from the parking station to the intersection of St Mary's Road, Prince Albert Road and College Street, in the front of the Cathedral. Privately owned parking stations in other parts of the city are more expensive than the Domain.

Take notice of the closing times of the Domain station because there is a fine of $40 if you have to ring the emergency number on the parking ticket and get someone to open the station and retrieve your car.

City Centre

Though principally a shopping area, there are a few sites worth visiting.

Martin Place

A traffic thoroughfare until 1973, Martin Place, or Martin Plaza as it is sometimes called, is a wide pedestrian mall that stretches for five blocks, from George Street to Macquarie Street. At the George Street end near the GPO is **the Cenotaph,** where a Military Memorial Ceremony takes place on the last Thursday of the month at 12.30pm. On other Thursdays the Army Band plays near the monument. It is near the Cenotaph that Sydney's official Christmas Tree is erected. Now an artifical thing!

Between Pitt and Castlereagh Streets, near the *MLC Centre*, there is a sunken amphitheatre where free lunchtime entertainment is staged Mon-Fri, noon-2pm.

Near the Elizabeth Street crossing is Halftix, where you can pick up half-priced tickets for that evening's theatre performances.

The entrance to Martin Place Railway Station is between Phillip and Macquarie Streets.

Sydney Tower

The Tower soars over 300m above the city, and is the highest public building in the Southern Hemisphere. It is located above the Centrepoint Shopping Complex, bounded by Pitt, Market and Castlereagh Streets. From the Market Street foyer take the lift to the Podium Level, then board one of three double-decker lifts that will take you to the Observation Level (Level 4). Here there are high-powered binoculars, an illuminated display of Sydney Harbour's water traffic, a tourist booking and information service, audio and guided tours.

Level 3 has the highest coffee lounge in Australia; Level 2 has a self-service revolving restaurant; and Level 1 has an a la carte up-market restaurant.

The Observation Level is open daily 9.30am-9.30pm, Sat til 11.30pm.

The Queen Victoria Building

There is more information on this restored building in the Shopping chapter, but even if you aren't interested in shopping, you should call in and have a look. It is not just a shopping centre, it is a remarkable building, with Style.

Sydney Town Hall

Situated on the corner of George and Druitt Streets, the Town Hall was built between 1868 and 1889 in French Renaissance style. Its concert hall houses a pipe organ which ranks with the biggest and best in the world. The Sydney City Council administrative offices occupy the modern tower block at the rear of the building. The Town Hall was given a face-lift in time for Sydney's Sesquicentenary in 1992. Prior to 1842, Sydney had not received city status.

Centrepoint Tours conduct tours of the building when there are no functions taking place, so ph 9231 4629 for further information. When available the tours begin at 10.30am, run for 1 3/4 hours, and cost $10 per person.

Town Hall Railway Station has entrances to the underground on both sides of George Street.

St Andrew's Cathedral

The Cathedral has twin towers reminiscent of York Minster, and is the oldest cathedral in Australia. The foundation stone was laid on May 17, 1837 by Governor Bourke. Work stopped in 1842 due to lack of funds, as the colony had financial problems because of a three year drought. The Cathedral was finally completed in 1868.

There was a lot of drama during its construction, including a change of architects, and the inside of the church had to be completely turned around as in the original plans, the back door opened onto the main George Street. It is possible to buy a book detailing the history of this beautiful Cathedral.

Cinema District

The next block on George Street, between Bathurst and Liverpool Streets, has four cinema complexes, the local branch of Planet Hollywood, a couple of McDonald's, a Pizza Hut, and other varieties of fast food outlets. There are also pinball parlours, restaurants and coffee shops. In short, this is a very busy part of the city.

Chinatown

Continue down George Street, turn right at Goulburn

Street, and first on the left will bring you to Chinatown, which has the usual amount of restaurants, delicatessens and herbalists.

From here it is a short walk to Paddy's Markets, the Entertainment Centre, or the restored Capitol Theatre.

Darling Harbour

Darling Harbour is Sydney's newest area, and is nearly half the size of the Sydney Business District at 54ha (133 acres). It was originally a shipping and storage area for the Port of Sydney, but the advent of container ships sounded its death knoll and it became nothing more than an eyesore. After years of planning, wrangling amongst civic authorities, and the investment of millions of dollars, Darling Harbour has become one of the entertainment centres of Sydney. On weekends families can be seen strolling along the walkways, picnicing on the grass and just having a good time.

There is always something on at Darling Harbour. Every weekend there is some program of entertainment, and almost every yearly festival or show has changed its venue to this central area - the Home Show, the Boat Show, Navy Week, Music Festivals, Book Fairs, Antique Fairs, the list goes on. For information on special events when you are in town, phone the Darling Harbour Infoline on 1902 260 568, or contact the information centre daily 9am-5pm, ph 9286 0111.

How to Get There
By Monorail, the closest station to the Pitt Street Mall is near the corner of Pitt and Market Streets. The monorail operates from 7am Mon-Fri, from 8am Sat-Sun.
By Rocks-Darling Harbour Shuttle Bus, which runs daily at 20 minute intervals, 10am-5.30pm, from Circular Quay along George St. to the Aquarium and Harbourside.
By Bus no 456 from Circular Quay via Town Hall to Darling Harbour, Mon-Fri 10am-2.30pm, Sat-Sun 11.30am-5pm, every 30 minutes.
By Sydney Ferries from Circular Quay to the Aquarium, via Balmain. The trip takes 22 minutes, and ferries leave every 30 minutes from Wharf 5. Matilda Cruises also run

The Monorail at Darling Harbour

ferries from Circular Quay to the Aquarium and adjacent to Harbourside, leaving every 30 minutes 10.15am-5pm ($3.10 per trip).

By Sydney Explorer Bus, which stops at Harbourside and the Chinese Gardens.

By Train - the nearest stations are Town Hall, from where you can walk down Market or Bathurst Streets then across Pyrmont Bridge; and Central Station, from where you can catch Bus 469, or take any bus travelling north along George Street and alight at Chinatown.

Parking
Although several thousand car parking spaces are available on the western side of Darling Harbour off Quay Street, adjacent to the Sydney Entertainment Centre; off Murray Street behind Harbourside; and off Darling Drive under the Sydney Exhibition Centre, it is an expensive operation to park your car for a whole day, so the best advice is to leave the car at home, or at a railway station on the outskirts of the city.

Getting around Darling Harbour
Of course, you can walk from attraction to attraction, but if you have small children, or elderly people with you, there are a couple of alternatives.

The People Mover train operates daily to all parts of the site, with major stops at the Aquarium, The Chinese Garden and Harbourside - $2.50 adults, $1.50 children.

Jolly Boat Rides operate a shuttle service Sat-Sun and school and public holidays, 11am-4pm, between the Aquarium steps and Harbourside - $2 adults, $1 children.

Taxis

If you have overstayed your visit and missed all the public transport available, there is always the option of grabbing a cab.

Taxi Ranks are located at the Convention Centre entrance (rear of Harbourside off Darling Drive), in front of Sydney Entertainment Centre, and at all the hotels.

Darling Harbour Super Ticket

Several of the attractions at Darling Harbour have banded together to offer reductions in the form of the Darling Harbour Super Ticket, which can be purchased at any of the information booths at Darling Harbour, the Sydney Aquarium, the Monorail, the Chinese Garden, or at Matilda Cruises. The cost is $29.9 adults, $19.50 children under 12, which sounds a bit expensive, but this is what you receive:

A two hour Matilda Harbour Cruise.

Entry to Sydney Aquarium.

A ride on the Monorail.

A visit to the Chinese Gardens.

Lunch at the Shark Bite Restaurant at the Aquarium.

When you add all that, the ticket is definitely worth considering. Also, all sections of the ticket can be used on the one day, or you can used some sections on that day, and the rest are good for one month from the date of issue. The ticket also has a few optional extras, such as discount on the People Mover and on the bus fare to Homebush Bay.

Now that you know how to get there, how to get around, how to leave, and all about the Super Ticket, let's see what there is to see and do.

Sydney Aquarium

The Aquarium is located near the city end of Pyrmont Bridge, and is one of the largest and most spectacular in the world. The numerous tanks and tunnels allow the visitor to experience life on the ocean floor, with hundreds of different species of marine life. There are also displays of river systems, crocodiles, rocky shores, and the Great Barrier Reef. A touch pool allows you to finally get your hands wet.

The Aquarium is open daily 9.30am-9pm, and admission is $14.90 adult, $7 child, $34.90 family (2 adults and up to 3 children), ph 9262 2300. The Shark Bite Restaurant has plenty to tempt your taste buds while you are here.

Australian National Maritime Museum

The museum, at the western end of Pyrmont Bridge, is dedicated to helping people understand and enjoy Australia's ongoing involvement with the sea. Among craft moored at the museum are yachts, warships, tugboats, and a refugee boat.

Free guided tours of the Museum building are available at regular intervals throughout the day, and booking must be made at the Information Counter on arrival. Audio tours are also available from the Information Counter - $3 adults, $5 for 2 adults sharing, $2 children.

The museum has a program of changing exhibitions, and information can be obtained by phoning the recorded information Hotline 0055 62 002 (time charged), or for general information, ph 9552 7777. There is also a library, a kiosk on the waterfront, and a shop with a wide range of nautical gifts. The museum is open daily 10am-5pm, and general admission is $7 adult, $4.50 child, $18.50 family. There are extra charges for special exhibitions.

Harbourside

Harbourside Darling Harbour is a shopping centre with 200 shops that include 54 waterfront restaurants and food places. There are no department stores, and many of the shops sell for the tourist trade although there are branches of fashion outlets that seem to find their way into every shopping centre in Sydney.

Harbourside shops have longer trading hours than in

any other complex in the city - Mon-Sat 10am-9pm, Sun 10am-6pm - the restaurants, of course, stay open longer.

Harris Street Motor Museum

The building next to Harbourside is the **Convention Centre**, and for people that are interested in cars, motoring and associated memorabilia, their next stop would be the Australian Motor Vehicle Museum, 320 Harris Street, a short walk from the Convention Centre Monorail Station. Here there is a spectacular array of classic machines from the earliest to the latest, with lots of hands-on exhibits, in an historic old Woolstore building. The museum and carpark cover almost 4ha on two levels. It even has a place where you can 'park' the kids for a while under supervision. *The Cadillac Cafe* is available for roadside snacks, and the bookshop stocks everything ever written about cars, and some out-of-the-ordinary souvenirs. The museum is open daily 10am-5pm, and **admission is $8 adults, $4 children**, ph 9552 3375.

The Powerhouse Museum

While you are in Harris Street, you should walk away from the water to no 500 and The Powerhouse Museum, Australia's largest museum. Created from the shell of an old Sydney power station, the museum is alive with dynamic exhibitions, hands-on fun and special performances. There is so much to see that some people spent the whole day wandering through this incredible exhibition. Tours, talks, films, performances, demonstrations and workshops are continually happening, and there is the *Ken Done Restaurant* (painted by guess who?) and a kiosk when you need sustenance. As always, there is a souvenir/book shop, but this one offers some way-out merchandise. The Powerhouse Museum is open daily 10am-5pm. Admission ia $5 adults, $2 children, under 5 free, ph 9217 0444.

Back at Darling Harbour proper, the **Exhibition Centre** is the next group of buildings, and information on the

Facing Page: Kids in the park-summer [top], winter [below]; (Overleaf) Two views of the Museum of Sydney on the site of the first Government House; the Facade [top], Edge of the Trees by Janet Lawrence and Fiona Foley in the forecourt with the restaurant[below].

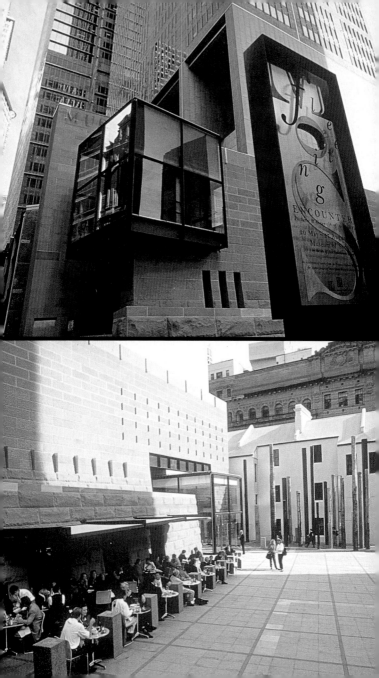

current shows is available from the Infoline.

In front of the centre is **Tumbalong Park**, and from there it is a short walk to the next attraction.

The Chinese Garden

The Garden was specially designed by landscape architects from Guangdong Province, and is the largest and most elaborate outside China. It covers a full hectare, and has a two-storey pavilion above a system of lakes and waterfalls. It is a serene retreat from the madcap and mayhem of the waterfront.

The Garden is open daily 8.30am-sunset and admission is $3 adults, $1.50 children, $6 family.

Across Pier Street from the Chinese Garden is the more than one hundred years old **Pumphouse Tavern and Brewery** (which is going to be demolished to make way for more development), and next to that is the **Sydney Entertainment Centre**. Chinatown is opposite the main entrance to the Centre, in Harbour Street.

From the Chinese Garden walk back towards the waterfront, and you will come to the newest attraction. Opened 1997, **Darling Walk** has 20,000 sqm, and half of that space is taken up by **Sega World**, Australia's first indoor theme park. Attractions here include a rollercoaster, theatre and live performances, and 'multimedia participation experiences'. To find out more about Sega World, ph 9264 5555.

Other attractions at Darling Walk are restaurants and shops that are 'interactive'.

Panasonic IMAX Theatre

There is no way you could miss the building - it is the strangely shaped one painted with yellow and black squares. The theatre has a 900 sqm movie screen, the largest in the world, and seating for over 500 people, and programs include documentaries on Antarctica and the Ocean. Current showings are advertised in the daily newspapers on the same pages as the more conservative cinemas. Admission is $13.95 adults, $9.95 children.

The top floor has the Star Grill Restaurant, run by one

Imax Theatre with the Marina at Darling Harbour in the foreground.

of Sydney's best-known chefs, Neil Perry (Rockpool and MCA Cafe). For more information, ph 9267 3101.

Kings Cross

The Cross is sleazy, of that there is no doubt, with its strip joints, sex shops and ladies of the night. But, if you drive through during the day mid-week, it may seem like any other suburb. It is at night that it comes into its own. There are some excellent restaurants and night spots, and there are some places where you have to be brave to enter. It is not the type of place where you talk to strangers, and believe me, there are some strange people walking the streets. Nevertheless, there are people would not think they had seen Sydney if they hadn't been to the Cross. It is a haven for backpackers because of the number of cheap hostels, and it is certainly a central area, but I wouldn't think of staying there if I was travelling with children.

Having said that, there are a couple of landmarks. The

El Alamein Fountain, on the corner of Darlinghurst Road and Macleay Street, was built to commemorate the men of the Australian 9th Division who fought in North Africa during World War II. It is an unusually shaped ball of a fountain, and there are always hundreds of people in the park surrounding it.

A short walk away, although in a different suburb, is *Elizabeth Bay House*, at 7 Onslow Avenue, **Elizabeth Bay**, ph 9356 3022. It was built for the Colonial Secretary, Alexander Macleay and his wife Eliza, and is presently furnished to the period, 1839-1845. In its day it was considered to be the finest house in the colony, and its views over the harbour would have been even more impressive then than they are now. It is a two-storey house with a grand winding staircase, and is maintained by the Historic Houses Trust. It is open Tues-Sun (Monday when a public holiday) 10am-4.30pm (except Christmas Day and Good Friday) and admission is $5 adult, $3 child, $12 family.

Sydney Jewish Museum
The museum is on the corner of Darlinghurst Road and Burton Street, south of Kings Cross Station, and is open Mon-Thurs 10am-4pm, Fri 10am-2pm, Sun 11am-5pm (closed Saturday and Jewish Holidays). Admission is $6 adult, $3 child, $15 family, ph 9360 7999.

The exhibits are spread over three floors with six mezzanine levels. The ground floor has a recreation of George Street in the 1840s, showing the homes and businesses of some of the Jewish settlers. There are also displays of elements of contemporary Jewish ritual, with guides available to answer any questions, and information on some famous Jewish Australians. The mezzanines contain the permanent exhibition of The Holocaust, and survivor volunteers are present on each level to offer a rare insight into the displays.

The museum has a shop with a wide range of souvenirs, and on the lower ground floor the excellent Cafe Macc offers traditional European and Israeli cuisine at reasonable prices.

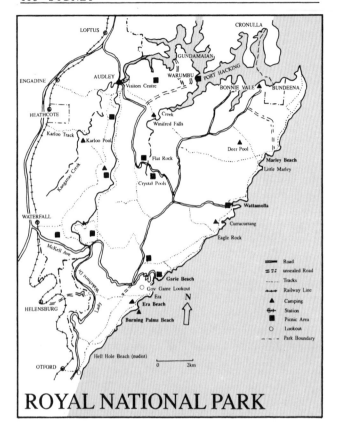

ROYAL NATIONAL PARK

Royal National Park

Royal National Park was gazetted in 1879 as 'The National Park', and was the first public reserve in Australia to be so termed. In fact, the Park can lay claim to being the first in the world, because although Yellowstone Park in the USA was established in 1872, it was not officially gazetted as a national park until 1883. When Queen Elizabeth II first visited Australia in 1954, she bestowed the title 'Royal', but most Sydneysiders still refer to it as 'The National Park'.

The Park is situated south of Port Hacking, about 29km from the centre of Sydney, and covers 16,000ha of vegetation and landscape typical of the Sydney Basin sandstone.

The original inhabitants of the area were the Aboriginal people of the Dharawal tribe, who used the sandstone caves for shelter and lived off the land and waterways. Little detail is known of their lifestyle as rock engravings, axe-grinding grooves, charcoal drawings and hand stencils are the only physical remains of the culture.

The Royal National Park was established by the then NSW Premier, Sir John Robertson, who saw a need for a recreation space for Sydney, many parts of which had become infested with vermin and disease.

Audley was the site of the first European settlement in the Park. The native mangroves and mudflats were replaced by grassed parkland and exotic trees, and added to the local fauna were deer, rabbits and foxes.

Park Features

The Park has been shaped from a sloping sandstone plateau, which rises from sea level at Jibbon Point in the north, to over 300m at Bulgo in the south.

The Park scenery is magnificent and varied. The waves from the open sea have produced majestic cliffs, broken every now and then by small creeks and beaches. Deep river valleys have been formed by streams flowing north to Port Hacking and east to the Pacific Ocean. The upper slopes have woodlands that merge with the heath vegetation on the plateaux. Gorges and valleys have forest and rainforest, the tidal channels of the rivers have mangrove, and the swamps are covered in sedges.

There are **numerous grassy areas** along the **Hacking River valley**, and from July to November the plateaux become a riot of colour from the wildflowers. There are **waterfalls** at *Wattamolla, Curracurrong, Uloola* and *National Falls.*

How to Get There

By Rail

Trains on the Illawarra-Cronulla line stop at Loftus, Engadine, Heathcote, Waterfall and Otford, and from these stations there are walking tracks into the Park.

By Car

From Sydney, follow the signs toward the **Airport**, and then follow the signs to Wollongong (Princes Highway) or President Avenue at *Brighton-le-Sands*, turn right and at the end of the street turn left onto Princes Highway keep going to you are past Sutherland. The Audley entrance to the Royal National Park is well signposted. You take a left turn of the Princes Highway just south of Sutherland.

From Liverpool City, take the Heathcote Road exit from the M5 motorway (before the toll booth). Turn right into Heathcote Road so you cross over the M5 Motorway and follow it all the way to the Princes Highway (between Engadine and Heathcote).

You can then do one of two things:

turn left and go back about 3km to enter the Park south of Sutherland (Audley entrance);

or turn right and head south to Waterfall and enter the Park there, about 1km north of the tollway.

From Wollongong, drive north along the Princes Highway. After reaching Bulli continue along Lawrence Hargraves Drive (don't go up the escarpment). Another way is to follow the Mt Ousley Road to the Princes Highway and turn right at Stanwell Tops to go to Stanwell Park. At the top of the Bluff, turn left along Lady Wakehurst Drive, then continue to the Otford entrance of the Park.

By Ferry

Cronulla National Park Ferry Cruises, ph 9523 2990, have a service from the wharf near Cronulla railway station to Bundeena, and the trip takes 25-30 minutes. The first ferry from Cronulla leaves at 5.30am Mon-Fri on the hour to 6.30pm, 8.30am Sat-Sun and public holidays on the hour to 6.30pm. The last ferry leaves Bundeena daily at 7pm (summer), 6pm (winter).

NB It should be noted that Bundeena is not within Royal National Park.

Tourist Information

A *Visitor Centre and Wildlife Shop* is on Farnell Avenue 100 metres past the entrance station. Call into the centre for advice on all aspects of your park visit. Permits are obtained here. Open daily 8.30am-4pm, ph 9542 0648. The shop sells books, film, maps, posters, gifts and souvenirs.

Park Entrance Fee

There is no charge for traffic travelling through and not stopping in the Park from Sutherland to places south of the Park.

For those that intend to stop within the park the following charges apply:

Bus - $3.00 per adult, $1.00 for each school age child, Under the age of 5 free, pensioners free. Must display pensioner card.

Cars - $9.00 per vehicle

Motor Bikes - $3.00 per bike

There is no charge for people who hike into the park for the day.

Park Regulations

All fauna, flora, Aboriginal sites and rock formations are protected.

Wildfires can destroy lives and property, so be careful, especially during the bushfire danger period (normally October to March). Use only the fireplaces provided and observe Total Fire Bans. Portable fuel stoves are required for camping.

Pets and Firearms are not permitted in national parks.

Vehicles, including motorbikes must keep to formed public roads. Drive carefully.

Please use rubbish bins if provided; or take rubbish with you when you leave the park.

Camping

Caravans and car camping are permitted at the camping ground at *Bonnie Vale*, off Bundeena Road. It has toilet and shower blocks, but no powered sites. In fact, there are only 40 sites in all, and during school holidays and long weekends, ballots are held to allot them. There are so many applicants that this seems to be the fairest way. At other times there is not so much demand, and therefore there is a good chance of securing a site, but booking ahead is essential.

For reservations, ph 9542 0648.

Site fees are: $10 per person for the first two people, and $2.00 extra per person over 5 years of age.

Children under 5 years of age are free.

There are lots of places for bush camping throughout the park, however booking and obtaining permits are essential, ph 9542 0648. The permits must first be obtained from the Visitor Centre. The permits are free, but written on the back of them are the special conditions that apply to camping in a national park, and this is the best way of making sure that everyone is aware of them.

Activities

Weekends see many organised picnics arranged by sporting clubs, church groups, etc, and family picnics with the addition of aunts and uncles, grandparents, etc, taking advantage of the wide open expanse near the Audley causeway.

National Park Ranger guided activities are available. Bookings and more information can be obtained by phoning 9542 0649.

Picnicking

There are many picnic areas dotted throughout the park, but there are only barbecue facilities at Audley, Warumbul, Wattamolla, Bonnie Vale and Garie. Kiosks are found at Audley, Wattamolla and Garie Beach.

Swimming

Safe salt water swimming is available at *Bonnie Vale, Jibbon, Wattamolla* and *Little Marley* beaches, and these are favourite spots for families.

Surfers head for *Garie, Era* and *Burning Palms* Beaches, which are patrolled by surf lifesavers on weekends and public holidays in summer.

Freshwater swimming is possible at *Blue Pools, Karloo Pool, Deer Pool, Curracurrang* and *Crystal Pools*, but care should be taken when swimming in rock pools. The water always tends to be cold, so it is easy to get cramps. It is not always easy to judge how deep a rock pool is, so it is best not to jump or dive into these pools. Spinal injury units of hospitals are always warning people about the dangers of diving into unknown waters.

Boating

The boatshed at Audley, ph 9545 4967 has rowing boats, canoes and aquabikes for hire, and only these may be used in Kangaroo Creek, and in the Hacking River above the causeway. Private boats, etc, can be used downstream of the Audley causeway.

The boat shed is open Mon-Sat 9am-5pm, Sun and public

holidays 9am-5.30pm. **The hiring fee for row boats, canoes and kayaks is $24 per day or $12 per hour.**
Two hour hire or half a day [9am-1pm; 1pm-5pm] hire is $18. Aquabikes cost $10 per half hour. A refundable deposit of $10 is required for each craft.

Walking

The Park has over 150km of walking tracks that provide access to the wide range of scenery available, and the Visitor Centre has track pamphlets. Bungoona, Governor Game and Otford Lookouts offer chances to take spectacular photos, and National, Winifred and Curracurrong Falls are easily accessible.

Cycling

The best route for cyclists is Lady Carrington Drive, which is closed to motor vehicles, and is relatively flat. Ask at the Visitor Centre for directions. Bicycles and mountain bikes are only allowed on management trails. They arre not permitted on walking tracks.

If you are visiting the Royal National Park on a Sunday or Wednesday, you might like to check out **The Sydney Tramway Museum** in Pitt Street, Loftus, ph 9542 3646. It is open Sun 10am-5pm, Wed 9.30am-3.30pm, but no one is admitted in the hour prior to closing.

Trams operated in Sydney for one hundred years to 1961, and a fleet of over 1500 vehicles provided the city with an efficient transport service. The Sydney Tramway Museum has an excellent collection of Sydney trams, and others from Brisbane, Ballarat, Melbourne and San Francisco, and also a selection of the buses which replaced them in Sydney. This fleet includes the last remaining double deck trolley bus.

Every open day, a number of the museum's trams operate along a kilometre of track, each return trip taking about 15 minutes, but the San Francisco PCC Streetcar only operates on the first Sunday of the month. There is also a tramway waiting shed from Railway Square, the unique counterweight dummy from the Balmain line, and an extensive range of photographs and artifacts.

The museum has a shop with a range of books, post cards, video tapes and souvenirs, as well as snacks and drinks. There are also picnic facilities within the Museum grounds.

Admission is $10 adult, $5 child, and includes unlimited tram rides and use of facilities.

Index to Maps

Photography Credits

© C. Burfitt, facing title page, p5, facing p16, facing p41, p76, facing p89 [below], p92, p101, p109, facing p112 [top], p114.

© Little Hills Press; Eduard Domin, Photographer facing p17, facing p89 [top], facing p112 [below].

© Tourism New South Wales, cover, back cover, facing p40, facing p56, facing p88.

© QVB Management facing p57.

© Museum of Sydney, facing p113.

Index

Another great travel title by
Little Hills Press

See our Home Page
http://www.littlehills.com

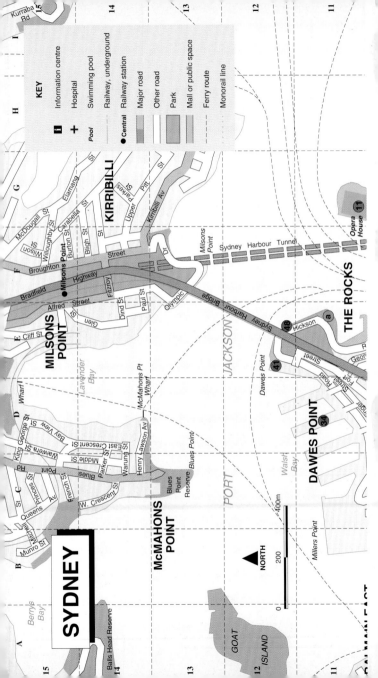